THE MACEOS

── and the ──

FREE STATE OF

GALVESTON

THE MACEOS
and the
FREE STATE OF
GALVESTON

An Authorized History

KIMBER FOUNTAIN

THE
History
PRESS

Published by The History Press
Charleston, SC
www.historypress.com

First published 2020

Manufactured in the United States

ISBN 9781467143530

Library of Congress Control Number: 2019952116

For Eric, my partner in crime.

CONTENTS

ACKNOWLEDGEMENTS

First and foremost, I must acknowledge the Maceo family. When I first met Concetta Maceo, she had recently arrived on the island and was planning on attending nursing school, but something in me knew that she was right where she belonged, immersed in the modern incarnation of the family business, Maceo Spice and Import Company. She had no idea that I was already borderline obsessed with the Maceo history, but over the years she became a fan of my writing. Thus when she asked me to take on the task of telling the Maceo story, it was a dream come true. I am humbled and grateful to her for the invitation, because the world certainly needs to know about this remarkable group of people. I am beyond thrilled that I am the one who gets to share it.

To Vic, Ronnie, Frank and Marlina Maceo, thank you for your time and for sharing your stories with me. Your input was invaluable. And to the rest of the Maceo clan, living and deceased, whether I have met you or not, thank you for who you were and who you are and for contributing to such a fascinating history in your own way. I hope you have as much fun reading this as I had writing it.

This book would not have been possible without the help of my fiancé, Eric. Every couple has those little idiosyncrasies that make it work, and one of ours just happens to be a fascination with the history of organized crime. His brain is like a gangster encyclopedia, with knowledge surpassed only by the insane number of books he has on the topic. He was my co-investigator, helping me unravel the larger aspects of this story piece by piece, and without him, this book would not be what it is.

To D.B., the anonymous benefactor who let me spend hours photographing his wonderful collection of memorabilia from the Free State, thank you for helping me develop a visual component to this story that would never have existed without your assistance.

To my mom the English professor, who read to me every night as a child, without fail, that has made all the difference in my life. To my dad, who was so happy when I was old enough to accompany him to the gangster flicks and shoot-'em-ups that my mom did not want to go see. It may seem like the simplest thing, but it gave me a perspective and a love for this genre that I would not have had without him.

Lastly, sometimes soulmates have four paws and fur, and mine certainly does. Thank you, Elle, you make everything in life so beautiful.

INTRODUCTION

Several years ago, I happened upon an elderly man on the steps of Shearn Moody Plaza at the intersection of Twenty-Fifth Street and the Strand. I do not recall the exact circumstances of our meeting, but I do remember that he had just missed his bus. Even though I had lived in Galveston for only about a year and a half, I was already fully informed on the shortcomings of our public transit, so I offered him a ride. His destination was Walmart clear on the opposite side of town, but his faded clothes, worn shoes and soft face, punctuated by a gentle demeanor that reminded me of my late grandfather, pulled at my heartstrings, and I would have driven him all the way to Houston if he had asked.

At this point in my life, I knew little if anything about Galveston's history, and the island city was only beginning its dramatic, post–Hurricane Ike transformation. It was still a sleepy little town barely waking up from its disaster-induced hibernation. I listened in bewilderment, tinged with a touch of disbelief, as he described the Galveston that *he* remembered—a Galveston that, despite his age, was so clear in his memory that the city he lived in now was almost foreign. It was the Galveston that he first encountered while stationed at Fort Crockett in the 1940s.

As we drove down Seawall Boulevard, past the crumbling remains of the Flagship Hotel and what little remains of the fort where he had served, past vacant lots and developed lots full of vacant buildings, he spoke of ornate gambling houses and swanky nightclubs on every corner and a section of Postoffice Street that was brimming with bawdy houses. But most of all, he recalled a city teeming with wealth, glamour and prestige. His tone took a sharp turn as the mist lifted from his eyes and the illusion of grandeur recreated by his memories fell away, no longer concealing the scenes outside his window. He looked over toward the Gulf and remarked wryly, "You know, back then, if you'd told me that someday Galveston would be some obscure, family-friendly beach town, I never would have believed you."

When I dropped him off, he wrote down the address of his retirement home and told me to come see him sometime. I never did, and I have never regretted that more than I do now. In fact, I was dumbfounded by what he told me—the Galveston he described seemed so unreal that I dismissed it entirely. Even though I held on to his contact information for a long time with the intention of going to see him someday, I did not once recall the topic of our conversation until I began writing this book, seven years later.

Not long after this encounter, I was officially introduced to the history of the Maceo family and the era known as the Free State of Galveston. As it slowly revealed itself to me, I simultaneously discovered that the era had been more or less banished from the annals of conventional Galveston history. The city has no monuments to the Free State nor any museums that display its ephemera. Almost all of the Victorian houses along the island's primrose path have gone the way of the bulldozer, and the two that remain are in a state of abject ruin. All three of the resplendent dens of vice have been erased—one by water, one by fire and another in the name of progress.

Even more unfortunate, the recorded history of the era has been shattered, scattered and fragmented almost beyond recognition, so all that remains are multiple versions of the same recycled story that do not even begin to capture the essence of what was really happening in Galveston. I realized while writing this book that even I was guilty of this. I have written countless articles on this topic, and it was a key component of my first two books, but I admit that some information in this book contradicts what I have written prior. This is because we Galveston historians have unknowingly told and retold many stories about the Maceo Era that are *almost* right. It was quite the treasure hunt to trace the origins of those stories and uncover those intricate details that, when combined, present an entirely new perspective.

Despite these now corrected errors, one thing I have never done is marginalize the key characters of the Free State, as is so often the case. They are drawn as caricatures and painted with a Hollywood brush into portraits with labels like "gangster," "mobster" and "Mafia," but that sensationalistic view obscures a story that is far more fascinating. Fortunately, I had made up my mind about the Maceos long before I was confronted with this historical distortion. In fact, my initial reaction when I first began to uncover this history was, "Why is no one talking about this?" The way I interpreted it, Sam and Rose Maceo were nothing short of geniuses who had found a way to elevate a city to enormous prosperity during some of the bleakest decades in United States history. I did not see them as thugs or even as criminals; they were insatiable entrepreneurs and brilliant businessmen who just so happened to have a few undertakings that were illegal because of the government's misguided desire to legislate morality and a flawed system that perpetuates the notion that vices are crimes. (They are not.)

Furthermore, the economy created by the Maceo family was an explosive powerhouse that swept through the city and made everything sparkle, much unlike the accumulated wealth of the nineteenth century that was ultimately confined to a handful of elite families who choked out the competition. When the Maceos made money, everyone made money, and the Maceos' power was everyone's power. For four decades, through war and economic depression, Galveston was buttressed by an impenetrable financial fortress built on insanely clever management and steeled by compassion for the community.

The Maceos also appear to have protected Galveston from the sinister outside influences of American Mafia syndicates who, if allowed to assume control, would have been able to easily victimize the residents' laissez-faire look at life. Of course, the underworld does not keep public records, and documentation on this theory is sparse at best, but I was inspired by a quote from the obituary of Gary Cartwright, renowned historian, journalist and author of one of my favorite books on Galveston history, *Galveston: A History of the Island*. The *Austin American-Statesman* quoted former *Texas Monthly* publisher Mike Levy. He said of Cartwright, "Great writers do three things: get the stories—in other words, get people to talk, and Gary could get anybody to talk—then put all the pieces together and have the wisdom to figure out what it [means]." Like a fly fisherman bounding up the river, confident that a rock will be there when he steps, I followed the clues, and I have the utmost faith that my discernment led me to the right conclusion, even if the path along the way was a little dicey.

In addition to the speculation of questionable partnerships, the demise of the Maceo empire was another component that has led to its frequent omission from mainstream history. It began to weaken from within at the precise moment that the evolution of mainstream culture reached an apex of nonconformity and intolerance. It was a timeless clash between rebellion and compliance, a war between morality and legality, and we all know that the winners write history. So, this perfect storm of internal decline and nationwide embarrassment not only dismantled the Free State but also relegated its history to the back shelf, despite decades as Galveston's singular sustenance. By the time the historical pendulum began its predictable journey in the other direction, the chips had been cashed, and the Maceos were little more than a misunderstood memory.

Now, it is my distinct honor and privilege, at the invitation of the living members of the Maceo family, to set the record straight, to dust off the shame and ridicule, drop the sensationalized labels and let the story of the original sin city shine like it did so many years ago.

1

ONCE UPON A TIME IN SICILY

Success stories often use ancestral history as a mechanism of insight into how and why a person or family became who they were, but that is not the case with the story of Galveston's Maceo family. Instead, the social and political climate that permeated the family members' early experiences is predominantly useful in revealing who they were not. Historically, the Maceo family's native island of Sicily has been inhabited by people who made their own rules, sometimes out of sheer necessity. Likewise, in their comparatively brief existence, the people of Galveston have been of a similar mindset. Long before the Maceos arrived, the city was already in possession of a reputation for defying the odds and expectations of both man and Mother Nature. The geographic similarities of Sicily and Galveston are a large factor in the demographic likeness of these two islands; despite the immediate proximity of each to their respective mainland, the briefest of disconnections is still somehow enough to create a culture of isolation, a communal feeling of superiority and a loyalty reserved exclusively for insiders. However, beyond this nuanced underpinning of rugged independence, Sicily's history diverges drastically from that of Galveston and the Maceos, both of whom became quite content with living outside the law but would never capitalize on the Sicilian trademarks of extreme violence and vicious extortion.

For centuries, Sicily was a pawn in the political games of regimes and emperors with various interests in controlling the Mediterranean. With an inherent military value derived from its location in the heart of the Mediterranean Sea, Sicily was either conquered or bartered by Phoenicians,

Greeks, Etruscans, Carthaginians, Romans, Byzantines and Normans. It was then occupied by Arab, French, Spanish and Austrian armies before finally seeking union with Italy, which led to an invasion of its troops as well.[1] As advantageous as Sicily's land was to the maneuvering of power, this perpetual state of flux was equally as damaging to the people who lived there. Whipping boys of the state, Sicilians were constantly subjected to the endless whims and desires of whatever flag happened to be flying overhead at any given time. Each state had different rules and higher taxes but the same brutal law enforcement.

This violent suppression was made possible and perpetuated by a feudal system of government that was installed by the Romans and continued by their successors because of its ability to glean wealth for the aristocracy from the backbreaking labor of peasants who were granted no security or political influence.[2] The persistent oppression from tyrannical governments led to a rise in Sicilian nationalism and sharpened loyalties among fellow countrymen and especially families. Subsequently, it prompted the formation of *cosche*, regional tribes of Sicilians who allied for protection and a sense of solidarity within a fractured system.[3] From these clans arose a mentality that was described by one word that is thought to be derived from the Arabic words for "place of refuge."[4] The word is exclusive to the early language of Sicily, with a meaning that was originally a composite of excellence and bravery. Long before the word *mafia* was first hijacked by a secret society and then Americanized to reference an indistinct array of criminal enterprises, it was a mindset that indicated a powerful sense of individuality and a stoic willingness to resist corrupt government.[5]

Feudalism on the island was finally rescinded in 1812 while under the rule of Spanish Bourbon King Ferdinand, whose domain consisted of Naples and Sicily and was called the Kingdom of the Two Sicilies. Hearing news of a pending invasion by Napoleon Bonaparte, who was already fast approaching with his army, King Ferdinand fled his home in Naples and sought haven in the other half of his kingdom. Sicilian barons (who oversaw the working class but still had no claim to the land) negotiated a deal. In exchange for the king's protection, they sought reformation. They demanded the end of feudalism, a constitution and the right to own property.[6] Unfortunately, what initially appeared to be a massive victory for the Sicilian people ended up creating the perfect conditions for the suppressed to become the suppressor.

King Ferdinand decreed that the feudalist estates of Sicily's rural farmland would be private property. He then divided them equally among the barons.

Often preferring city life, the barons would lease their land to *gabelloti* (revenue collectors), many of whom were the leaders or organizers of a cosche. They oversaw operations and paid rent to the baron with a percentage of each harvest. In turn, they divided the estate into small parcels and rented them to tenant farmers. With the barons in the city and the peasants working the land, the gabelloti were the go-betweens. They soon realized that this new system erased all accountability from their position. Both the employers and employees were beholden to them, as was the urban food supply, and this allowed them to operate virtually unchecked. Before long, they found a way to parlay this position into profit, and both landowners and peasants became the victims of merciless exploitation at the hands of the gabelloti.[7] Those who resisted were murdered to ensure the cooperation of other targets. Extortion and *pizzu* (protection money) were inescapable facts of life when the price for freedom was death.[8]

In their original form, mafia clans had been sporadic bands of rebels, barons and field hands who protected the specific interests of their region, inspiring a reverence from commoners who believed that they were their only protection from outlaws, bandits and, worst of all, corrupt governments.[9] But greed, a propensity for violence and the willingness to murder to achieve a desired result made possible the manipulation of a weak system, which in turn merely increased the cosche quest for power. Although these original clans were never unified under a central command, their common goals eventually led to the organization of a secret society that exploited their name just as they did their people. The Mafia was born.[10]

In response, the mid-nineteenth century brought the emergence of Risorgimento, a movement that supported the unification of Sicily with Italy. Unity was likely seen by the Sicilian peasantry as having the potential to curtail the Mafia's ever-increasing power, and in 1860, the commoners offered an ecstatic welcome to Italian military leader and Risorgimento champion Giuseppe Garibaldi when he arrived on the island with one thousand volunteer troops. Called "red shirts" for their striking uniforms, Garibaldi's men were joined in their quest to take down the Spanish Bourbon monarchy by two thousand rebel farmers who poured in from all over the countryside. Their presence all but guaranteed victory for Garibaldi, who later dubbed them his *Squadri della Mafia*, or Mafia squadron. The story of Garibaldi and the rebels was immortalized in an 1863 play titled *Mafiosi della Vicaria* (*Heroes of the Penitentiary*), which portrayed them as subjugated yet heroic patriots. This dramatic portrayal was singlehandedly responsible for inserting the word *mafia* into the vernacular, although an 1868 Italian dictionary defined it as "bravado," revealing that the motives and tactics of the Mafia proper were yet unknown.[11]

Although the Mafia successfully presented itself under the guise of benevolent benefactors who were protecting their homeland and its people, the endgame was the accumulation of wealth and power. Soon after the unification was made official in 1861, common Sicilians found themselves disillusioned by the prospect of reformation as they looked around to find even more chaos than before Garibaldi arrived. Their Italian rulers were headquartered far away in northern Italy, and the lack of any sanctioned law enforcement or judiciary on the island caused the crime rate to increase by 87 percent in the decade after unification. In 1873, the Italian province of Lombardy recorded one murder for every 44,673 residents, while Sicily recorded one murder for every 3,194 residents. As the poverty level skyrocketed and conditions became increasingly desperate, the Italian government responded with well-intentioned but misguided totalitarian policies. This launched another upswing in nationalistic pride and reenergized the traditional Sicilian disdain for arbitrary authority.[12]

The Mafia became even more powerful as it seized the opportunity to extort payments from wealthy landowners and merchants for protection of the members' families and financial holdings. Its influence was also buoyed by those who were still convinced, despite the escalating bloodthirst and greed, that the Mafia was the only solution to a government that felt as foreign as any before it.[13] Even the Catholic Church allied with the Mafia to protect its expansive land investments and keep its laborers in line, and the clergy's gratitude made them unwilling to denounce the clans' gruesome tactics from the pulpit.[14] Up to this point, the Mafia's power had been self-proclaimed, but it was about to become official.

In 1874, the conservative leaders of the Italian government attempted to thwart the disastrous conditions in Sicily by sending troops to the island, but the troops' authoritarian actions instead caused an uprising that spread over all of Italy, resulting in a government collapse. For the first time in the country's history, the left wing assumed power and promptly incorporated forty-eight Sicilian deputy positions into the government. Almost all of them were claimed by mafioso. The transformation from renegade countrymen to legitimate politicians was complete, and the Mafia celebrated by adopting a ritual blood oath ceremony to further cement family allegiances. The oath was an honor code called *omerta*, which literally translates to "manliness" but implies far deeper meanings of loyalty to family and refusal to cooperate with government authority, choosing instead to enact personal justice. In 1887, the Mafia proved its absolute authority by violently squashing one of the first labor movements on the island. Progress had once again rendered itself impossible.[15]

Around this time, the United States initiated an open-door immigration policy that was especially enticing to Sicilians who wished to leave behind the economic and social atrocities of their island. Between 1890 and 1920, roughly four million Italian and Sicilian immigrants crossed the Atlantic Ocean on ships called lemon boats, because they transported citrus fruits as well as passengers.[16] Most of these were peasants with no ties to the organized outfits, and the others were either petty criminals on the run from the law or insignificant associates of the Mafia who were seeking to escape an impending retribution for some wrongdoing. The prominent figures and members in good standing among the Mafia families had no reason to leave—there was no need to cross an ocean and risk their lives to expand their enterprises, as they were quite satisfied with the roles that they had carved for themselves.[17]

The clans were headquartered in the rural territories, but the major hub of their undertakings, and thus one of the most crime-ridden areas in Sicily, was the city of Palermo on the northern coast. The sensuous tropical climate and cityscape dotted with majestic palm trees and fragranced with the aroma of blossoming citrus trees was a mere façade behind which corruption took its deepest root.[18] Members of the Mafia controlled all of the markets in Palermo and used the city streets to sell their rustled cattle and exploit merchants with their control of the food supply.[19] Palermo also happened to be the home of two families, the Maceos and Sansones, who were quickly growing weary of the turmoil in their native land. The alliance they forged was not an anomaly among Sicilian families, and although the exact circumstances that prompted it are not known, it manifested itself through marriage.

Vito Maceo (1854–1929), son of Tommaso Maceo (1826–1888) and Olivia (née Ferrara, born 1836), married Angelina Sansone (1863–1941), daughter of Rosario Sansone (1833–1915) and Mariana (née Serio, born 1842) on May 9, 1881. Vito's brother Vicenzo Maceo (1865–1939) married Angelina's sister Concetta Sansone (1867–1943) on November 10, 1887. The early hardships faced by these families in Sicily are evidenced by the untimely deaths of two young grandsons. Gaetano Maceo, son of Vito and Angelina, was born in 1892 and passed away at age five. Antonino Maceo, son of Vicenzo and Concetta, was born in 1895, and though records do

Above: Maceo family crest. *Family collection.*

Opposite: Sam Maceo's petition for naturalization. *Ancestry.com.*

not indicate the year of his death, his name was not listed on the passenger manifests when the family emigrated from Sicily just a few years later.[20]

Vito and Angelina were the first to set sail to the United States. They boarded the USS *Manilla* with Vicenzo, Rosario Sansone and their five remaining children, Olivia (1882–1949), Tommaso Frank (known as Frank, 1884–1918), Rosario "Rose" (1887–1954), Salvatore "Sam" (1894–1951) and Vincent C. (1896–1947).[21] Most accounts claim that this set of Maceos left Sicily in 1901, but when Salvatore submitted his application

No. M18

U. S. DEPARTMENT OF LABOR
NATURALIZATION SERVICE

UNITED STATES OF AMERICA

The statements contained herein constitute the record of the examination of the applicant and his witnesses made by me in accordance with the requirements...

M. Madison
U. S. Naturalization Examiner.

PETITION FOR NATURALIZATION

ORIGINAL

Ht 5 7
Color W
Comp. *dark*
Eyes *br*
Hair *black*
Marks *none*

To the Honorable the *District* Court of *U.S. S.D. of Texas* at *Houston* hereby filed, respectfully showeth:

First. My place of residence is *Co. "B" Training Det. SC College Station Tex*

Second. My occupation is *Soldier* (Give number, street, city or town, and State.)

Third. I was born on the *7th* day of *March* anno Domini 1894 at *Palermo* *Italy*

Fourth. I emigrated to the United States from *Palermo, Italy* on or about the *15* day of *Sept*

anno Domini 1 *907*, and arrived in the United States, at the port of *New Orleans La* on the *2* day of *Oct*

anno Domini 1 *907*, on the vessel *Mancello* (If the alien arrived otherwise than by vessel, the character of conveyance or name of transportation company should be given.)

Fifth. I declared my intention to become a citizen of the United States on the _____ day of _____ anno Domini 1 _____

at _____, in the _____ Court of _____

Sixth. I am *not* married. My wife's name is _____; she was born on the _____ day of _____, anno Domini 1

at _____, and now resides at _____

I have *no* children, and the name, date and place of birth, and place of residence of each of said children is as follows: (Give number, street, city or town, and State.)

This petition is filed under the provisions of the Act of Congress approved May 9, 1918

I entered the U.S. Army on *6/15/18* and am still in the Service.

Seventh. I am not a disbeliever in or opposed to organized government or a member of or affiliated with any organization or body of persons teaching disbelief in or opposed to organized government. I am not a polygamist nor a believer in the practice of polygamy. I am attached to the principles of the Constitution of the United States, and it is my intention to become a citizen of the United States and to renounce absolutely and forever all allegiance and fidelity to any foreign prince, potentate, state, or sovereignty, and particularly to *Victor Emanuel III King of Italy* of whom at this time I am a subject, and it is my intention to reside permanently in the United States.

Eighth. I am able to speak the English language.

Ninth. I have resided continuously in the United States of America for the term of five years at least immediately preceding the date of this petition, to wit, since the _____ day of _____ anno Domini 1 90 _____ Texas, and in the State of _____ continuously next preceding the date of this petition, since the _____ day of *July* anno Domini 1 908, being a residence within this State of at least one year next preceding the date of this petition.

Tenth. I have not heretofore made petition for citizenship to any court. (I made petition for citizenship to any _____ Court of _____ at _____, on the _____ day of _____ anno Domini 1 _____, and the said petition was denied by the said Court for the following reasons and causes, to wit _____, and the cause of such denial has since been cured or removed.)

Attached hereto and made a part of this petition are my declaration of intention to become a citizen of the United States and the certificate from the Department of Labor, together with my affidavit and the affidavits of the two verifying witnesses thereto, required by law. Wherefore your petitioner prays that he may be admitted a citizen of the United States of America.

Salvatore Maceo
(Complete and true signature of petitioner.)

Declaration of Intention No. _____ and Certificate of Arrival No. _____ from Department of Labor filed this _____ day of _____, 191 _____.

NOTE TO CLERK OR COURT.—If petitioner arrived in the United States ON OR BEFORE JUNE 29, 1906, strike out the words reading "and Certificate of Arrival No. _____ from Department of Labor."

AFFIDAVITS OF PETITIONER AND WITNESSES

United States of America
Southern District of Texas ss:

The aforesaid petitioner being duly sworn, deposes and says that he is the petitioner in the above-entitled proceedings; that he has read the foregoing petition and knows the contents thereof; that the said petition is signed with his full, true name; that the same is true of his own knowledge, except as to matters therein stated to be alleged upon information and belief, and that as to those matters he believes it to be true.

Salvatore Maceo
(Complete and true signature of petitioner.)

Lt E W Reagan occupation *Soldier* residing at *College Station*

and *Lt W H Bennett* residing at _____

each being severally, duly, and respectively sworn, deposes and says that he is a citizen of the United States of America; that he has personally known *Salvatore Maceo*, the petitioner above mentioned, to have resided in the United States continuously immediately preceding the date of filing his petition, since the *1st* day of *July* anno Domini 1918, and in the State in which the above-entitled petition is made continuously since the *1st* day of *July* anno Domini 1 918; and that he has personal knowledge that the said petitioner is a person of good moral character, attached to the principles of the Constitution of the United States, and that the petitioner is in every way qualified, in his opinion, to be admitted a citizen of the United States.

E W Reagan 2nd Lt S.C.R.C.
(Signature of witness.)

W H Bennett 2nd Lt Inf. R C
(Signature of witness.)

Subscribed and sworn to before me by the above-named petitioner and witnesses in the office of the Clerk of said Court this *16* day of *July* anno Domini 19 *18*.

L Crusteso, Clerk.

By _____, Deputy Clerk.

[OVER]

for naturalization years later, he recorded his arrival as October 2, 1902.[22] Vicenzo then returned to Sicily to escort his immediate family members on their voyage.

On April 21, 1904, Vicenzo stepped back onto the *Manilla* with his wife, Concetta, ten dollars and their five children, Olivia (1888–1941), Mariana (1891–1965), Frank Tommaso (also known as Frank, 1892–1964), Rosario Charles (1898–1987) and Vic C. (1903–1997). They were accompanied by Concetta and Angelina's mother, Mariana Serio Sansone, who was joining her husband. She had twenty dollars in her possession. Among all of them, only Vicenzo and his two daughters could read or write in any language.[23] They arrived in New Orleans on May 12, 1904.

The Big Easy was the preferred destination for most Sicilians who immigrated in the late nineteenth and early twentieth centuries. They endured a three-week journey in cramped quarters aboard a wooden sailing ship with no plumbing or running water. The average life expectancy in the United States was 47 years, and thirty dollars was barely more than one month's wages. Neither Maceo family knew anything about their future home—not the language or the people or that one day their sons would build an empire with an influence so dynamic and far reaching that its legacy is still tangible 120 years later.

Admittedly, the evidence is circumstantial, but what is known of the Maceos' early history is adequate to establish a substantial degree of certainty that they were not members of the Sicilian Mafia. Regardless, the peculiar mindset that they eventually developed, influenced but not overtaken by their heritage, would elevate them far above a stereotype. The Maceos would go on to embody the most favorable qualities of their ancestry—libertarianism, bravery, excellence, determination, organization and intelligence—but trade in the tactics of terrorism, extortion and racketeering for generosity, philanthropy and community. They would rarely resort to violence, and even when they did, it never defined them. They would use their heritage as common ground to forge valuable alliances, but they would be bound to no one. The level of class, sophistication and diplomacy they infused into an otherwise tawdry profession would grow to outrank that of any mafioso. Despite the labels thrust upon them, the raw, unadulterated version of who the Maceos were and what they accomplished when they stepped off that ship after the most uncomfortable three weeks of their lives, is enough to unequivocally prove that the Maceo vision was unlike anything the world had ever seen.

2

FROM THE BAYOU TO THE BEACH

After nearly six thousand miles and a month at sea, the next day's dawn broke to illuminate the skyline of New Orleans on the horizon, and a group of weary, ragged Sicilians filtered onto the deck to catch the first glimpse of their new home. Those final hours aboard the lemon boat must have felt like a lifetime as the passengers pulled into port filled with anxious anticipation and riddled with excitement and a touch of sorrow for the lives they had left behind. Once the ship was securely fastened to the dock, a customs agent came aboard to interrogate the travelers and make sure that none of them were mafioso.[24]

The influx of Sicilians to and through New Orleans rarely included prominent members of the Mafia, but a significant portion of the immigrant population consisted of low-level associates and petty criminals who had enough experience with the ruling clans to know exactly how they operated. Their relocation to the United States had relieved them of their past burdens, including the requirement to submit to the only authority they had ever recognized. The state-sanctioned laws of their new land meant nothing, and they considered themselves unfettered and free to reap the spoils of an industry to which they had only ever been the victim. By the turn of the twentieth century, New Orleans was inflamed in the corrupt dealings of men who desired wealth, notoriety and retribution for sins that the city itself had never committed.

The main target of these misplaced predators was their own people, to whom they would send a threatening letter demanding payment for protection. The Italian shopkeepers and restaurateurs would have a specified time to respond, after which they would receive one last warning. Should that warning not be heeded, they would be executed, usually with a sawed-off shotgun.[25] By 1900, the newly formed New Orleans Mafia, headed by Charles and Tony Matranga, had seized control of downtown's important French market and engaged in bloody, urban warfare in an attempt to unseat the Provenzano family, who controlled the wharves and docks. This resulted in the murder of the police chief, David Hennessy. When the nineteen members of the Matranga clan indicted for the incident were acquitted, the people of New Orleans rallied, stormed the jail where they were being held in protective custody and lynched eleven of the perpetrators.[26]

Thus, the two Maceo families discovered a city much like the one they had left half a world behind, but they fostered an unshakable determination to make the best of their new lives, and soon their American lineage began to take root. Shortly after Vito and Angelina arrived in New Orleans in 1902, they temporarily settled on an upper floor of a three-story building at Royal and Dumaine, above a furniture store where Vito and his boys worked.[27] Their oldest daughter, Olivia, married a fellow Sicilian transplant named Giuseppe (Joseph) Frances Fertitta in 1902. Back in Sicily, the Fertittas were also connected through marriage to the Maceo-Sansone alliance. Olivia moved from New Orleans to Leesville, Louisiana, located in the far western portion of the state, where Joseph had settled prior to their marriage. Olivia's mother Angelina and father Vito followed with all of her brothers and sisters, Frank, Rose, Sam and Vincent C., an indication that they were more than willing to leave the sullied city behind, just as they had done with their native island. In 1903, Olivia Fertitta gave birth to a daughter, and between 1903 and 1919, the Fertitta family grew to include two more daughters and six sons.[28] Joseph and Olivia Fertitta lived their entire lives in Leesville, as did several of their children, but three of their sons, Frank, Victor and Anthony Fertitta, eventually moved to Galveston and become key players in the Maceo empire.

The passenger list for the 1904 journey of Vicenzo and Concetta stated their destination as Leesville, where their brother and sister lived,[29] but they ultimately decided to make a home with their immediate family in New Orleans, where Vicenzo worked as a cabinet maker.[30] Their oldest daughter, also named Olivia, went to join the other set of Maceos in Leesville after her 1907 marriage to her cousin Tommaso Frank Maceo, Vito and Angelina's oldest son, who they called Frank. In 1908, Olivia gave birth to their only child, a son named Victor Anthony. Frank later followed his brother Rose

Frank Maceo's death certificate from 1918. *Ancestry.com.*

to Galveston, where he passed away in 1918 at the untimely age of thirty-four.[31] After his death, Olivia Maceo left Leesville to join family in Galveston with their son Victor, who was more than savvy enough to fill the void left by his father's passing. Victor's position among the Maceos in Galveston earned him the nickname Vic A. "Gigolo" Maceo. Frank's death prior to the rise of the island empire, coupled with the fact that he was called by the same name as his cousin, has led to much confusion from historians attempting to decipher the Maceo family lineage. He is often mistaken for his cousin Frank Thomas Maceo (1892–1964), the son of Vicenzo and Concetta, who became the third-largest investor in the family's Galveston businesses.

Frank Thomas remained in New Orleans until the mid-1920s, as did his mother, father and three younger brothers, Rosario Charles, Vic C. and Samuel T., or "Little Sammie," who was born in 1910, the final and only American-born child of Vicenzo and Concetta.[32] His sisters, Olivia (Maceo) and Marianna, had already moved to Galveston by the time Frank married Katie Lo Piccolo on March 1, 1913. The couple had five children, all born in New Orleans. Shortly after the youngest was born in 1924, Frank moved his wife and kids, as well as his mother, father and two of his brothers to Galveston to join the rest of their family. The lone exception was Rosario C., who moved to Beaumont, Texas, and continued the cabinetry trade learned by his father. He settled there permanently after marrying Giuseppa Josephine Fertitta (daughter of Joseph's brother Salvatore Fertitta) in 1919.

Back in Leesville, the federal census reveals that by 1910, the only child of Vito and Angelina who was left at home was their youngest son, Vincent. Within that same year, however, he followed his older brother Rose to Galveston, and the two were the first Maceos to be included as residents of Galveston in the city directory. In 1911, they were listed as sharing a room in a boardinghouse at 712½ Tremont (Twenty-Third Street).[33] History will never know exactly how Rose Maceo learned of Galveston, or why he decided to make a home in the quaint but thriving city on a sandbar. Perhaps the warm breeze and towering palm trees reminded him of his native Palermo, but his family seemed to trust his intuitive decision, and by 1913, his older brother Frank and father, Vito, had also moved to Galveston Island.[34] Rose's mother, Angelina, stayed behind in Leesville with her daughter Olivia Fertitta for a

The 1920 census listing the household of Vicenzo and Concetta Maceo in New Orleans. *Ancestry.com.*

Sam Maceo's World War I draft card. *Ancestry.com.*

time but eventually joined her husband and sons on the island. Over the next decade, all but two members (Olivia Fertitta and Rosario Charles) from both branches of the Maceo family would permanently relocate to Galveston.

Meanwhile, Rose's brother Salvatore "Sam" Maceo was, by all accounts, traipsing across Texas. His naturalization papers state that he moved to the Lone Star State in 1908, but he does not appear to have immediately joined his family in Galveston, despite widespread claims that he was a barber at the Hotel Galvez shortly after it opened in 1911. His World War I draft registration (circa 1917) lists his residence as San Antonio,[35] and on June 15, 1918, he joined the United States Army and went to basic training in College Station.[36] By this time, Rose had been working as a barber in Galveston for nearly eight years and held a chair in a shop at 314 Twenty-Fifth Street.[37] He had also married a young, Texas-born Italian named Minina "Minnie" Torregrosso who had moved to Galveston with her sister around the same time as Rose.[38]

On December 16, 1918, a mere ten days after the aforementioned death of Rose's older brother Frank, Minnie passed away in her home, surrounded by family. She was only twenty-four years old. Her obituary mentions the death of her eleven-year-old brother the day prior, indicating illness as the cause of her death.[39] Years later, Rose's reputation as the strong arm of the Maceo empire would be reinforced with a rumor that he brutally murdered his first wife and her lover, but no reports were made of a murder in the days surrounding Minnie's death. This tall tale was most likely a misinformed mash-up of a story involving Rose's younger brother Vincent, who had also married in the years following their arrival in Galveston. In 1921, Vincent and a family friend found the body of his wife, Madge Maceo, in a thicket of trees with her head bashed in. The case was never solved.[40]

The year 1918 was certainly not a pleasant one for the Maceo family, least of all for Rose. The death of his older brother, the enlistment of another and the death of his young wife and little brother-in-law had an incalculable impact on thirty-one-year-old Rose. As a child, he had suffered the death of his five-year-old brother Gaetano in Sicily, witnessed countless atrocities committed by the Mafia in his home city and risked his life on the hope of creating a better existence. Yet after nearly twenty years in the states, he was still eking out a living as a barber. At maybe the precise moment when he was about to lose all faith and hope in himself and his future, the words that Mother Cabrini said to his brothers and cousins swept in to comfort him.

Saint Frances Cabrini founded the Missionary Sisters of the Sacred Heart of Jesus and moved to New Orleans in 1892 to serve at the mission she established there, one of sixty-seven across the nation. She was a devotee of the downtrodden, with a special place in her heart for the Italian immigrants in New Orleans, and family history maintains that the various Maceo children once found themselves the objects of her compassion. They were outcasts in New Orleans, poor, destitute and the regular targets of intense discrimination from the native residents who considered all Sicilians to be mafioso.[41] One day she said to them, "I know you are poor now, but it will not always be this way. You must have faith, and courage, and one day you will find a way to live your best life."[42]

Exactly one month after the death of Rose's first wife, on January 16, 1919, the United States Senate ratified the Eighteenth Amendment to the Constitution, which enacted a nationwide ban on the production, distribution, sale and consumption of alcohol. The national decree may have removed the supply, but it was powerless to mitigate the demand, and Prohibition spurred the meteoric rise of an underground economy that would put Rose and his brother Sam on the path to delivering wealth and prosperity to his family and an entire city population.

3

THE NOBLE EXPERIMENT

Despite the vagueness surrounding Sam's residence during the Maceo family's first years in Galveston, he is definitively known to have moved to the island after his brief service in the U.S. Army. The undisputed commonality between early historical accounts is that he and Rose were in fact barbers, and the tonsorial trade is what led to their introductions to Dutch Voight and Ollie Quinn. The most popular version of the story places Rose in a barber's chair at Murdoch's Bathhouse (Twenty-Third Street and Seawall Boulevard) and Sam at a barbershop inside the Hotel Galvez (Twenty-First and Seawall), both serendipitously located within the territory of the Beach Gang led by Voight and Quinn. Other versions attest that Sam and Rose owned a barbershop downtown on Market Street, and this is where the four became acquainted, which aligns more closely to the information recorded in city directories and Rose's draft card. Regardless of the geography, their acquaintance with the known gang leaders most likely took time and nurturing from Sam and Rose to develop into the professional relationship it eventually became.

Dutch and Ollie's business required the utmost trust and loyalty, something that was not merely handed over to a barber they barely knew. Fortunately for Sam and Rose, they each had an innate ability to create a welcoming and insulated environment for two of the most famous men in Galveston, silently foaming and shaving and snipping, making their customers feel at ease to speak openly and interjecting polite and informal conversation only often enough to be respectful. They always accommodated the expectation that shop talk would stay in the shop. While the Maceo brothers were slowly cultivating a relationship inside the building, outside the building, circumstances were percolating to create the perfect conditions for that relationship to blossom.

The city of Galveston has always been characterized by an endearing arrogance. Arrogant because it deserves to be, as few populations have endured the disasters—both natural and man-made—that the island has weathered and endearing because it has always translated these setbacks into triumph. In the first decade of the Maceos' island residency, Galveston had already left behind some of its greatest accomplishments, such as rivaling Ellis Island as the largest port of immigration in the United States in the late nineteenth century. This led to a demographic that was diverse, tolerant and already somewhat suspicious of a federal government that was beginning its first attempts at legislating morality by banning gambling and slowly succumbing to the temperance movement.[43] Galveston had also completed the mammoth grade-raising in 1911, which elevated the grade of the entire southern half of the city by an average of thirteen feet.

On the other side of the island, along the harbor, the Port of Galveston had built the most technologically advanced wharves in the world after the 1900 storm obliterated the docks and nearly one-fifth of the population, but it began a slow, torturous decline from atop the list of prominent U.S. ports when the Houston Ship Channel opened in 1914. The city would have sunk if it had not been for the Seawall and its subsequent boulevard. Completed in 1904 but extended several times over ensuing decades, the Seawall was initially installed as a protective measure and a companion to the grade-raising, but the famous sidewalk by the sea quickly became a popular attraction. By the time Galveston's commercial enterprises began to falter, investments along Seawall Boulevard had ballooned, and the city was well on its way to becoming an entertainment destination. Naturally, the entertainment in such an enterprising city as Galveston was not limited to seashore sundries, and despite policies passed by the city government that outlawed gambling, an organized poker operation sprang up around 1910.[44]

The operation was led by Oscar Ernest Voight (1888–1986), whose ancestry earned him the nickname "Dutch," an Americanized version of *Deutsch*, the German word for "German." He was also named the father of organized gambling in Galveston,[45] but his gambling network became particularly potent when he joined with Oliver J. "Ollie" Quinn who opened the Deluxe Club at 2017 Postoffice Street[46] and became the unofficial lynchpin of early Galveston vice. He and Voight launched several other

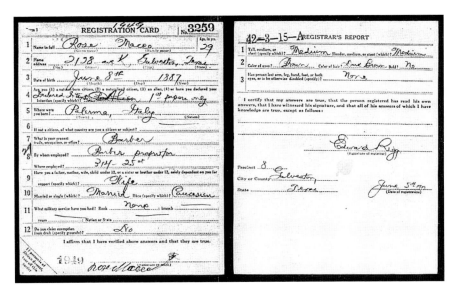

World War I draft card for Rose Maceo lists him as a "barber proprietor" at 314 Twenty-Fifth Street. *Ancestry.com.*

The Hotel Galvez was built in 1911 as a celebration of the completion of the grade-raising and a pronouncement of Galveston as a resort city. *Author's personal collection.*

gambling operations, most notably Mexican Joe's, the Little Club and the Greek American Club,[47] along with the Modern Vending Company that leased nickel-in-the-slot machines.[48] By day, the illicit business partners were pillars of the community. Quinn never missed a Sunday service at First Baptist Church, where he nonchalantly dropped $100 bills in the offering plate,[49] and Voight was described by Mayor Herbert Cartwright as being "such a likable guy that people were glad to let him put slot machines in their places of business."[50] They were laid-back and easygoing when it came to business and were generally accepting of competition. They were also committed to maintaining peace with rivals, and it was most likely their idea to divide the island into territories when a new set of underground entrepreneurs emerged in 1914.

The southern half of the island between Broadway Avenue and Seawall Boulevard became the domain of Dutch and Ollie's Beach Gang, and the area north of Broadway to the harbor was the designated territory of the newly formed Downtown Gang. Contrary to the stoicism exhibited by Quinn and Voight, the Downtown Gang was akin to its leaders, most aptly described by historian Gary Cartwright as "having considerably more guts than brains."

John Louis Nonus was born in Galveston in 1890, the son of Emanuel and Angelica Nonus, immigrants from Portugal. He was a scrappy fellow with an unwavering ambivalence toward authority, and both traits were sharpened by his family's abject poverty. When he made his foray into the underworld of Galveston, he changed his name to Johnny Jack Nounes so as not to sully his family posterity. Johnny Jack enjoyed street fights almost as much as he enjoyed breaking the law, and his defiant showmanship made him both a millionaire and a huge target for law enforcement. Gleaning most of his early wealth from prostitution and gambling, the pockets of his tailored designer suits from New York City bulged with rolls of $100 bills that he would graciously peel off for anyone in need.[51] Later in life, he grew weary of people asking for handouts and made an associate carry his money so that he had an excuse to decline their requests without technically lying.[52]

Johnny Jack's partner and fellow leader of the Downtown Gang was George Musey, who was of Syrian descent and born in Lake Charles, Louisiana. As more of a title than a nickname, he was also called "One-Armed George Musey," due to a partially amputated left arm. Musey worked as an automobile mechanic to support his family and was only fourteen years old when he first partnered with Nounes. His youth and inexperience were compensated by a brazen ambition and a penchant for violence that would later help him secure important connections in New Orleans. His ferocity was best illustrated by a gruesome murder that involved burying his victim face-down in quicklime.[53] George and Johnny Jack did their best to abide by Ollie and Dutch's diplomatic approach to business on the island but were instigators quite often, and territorial battles and slayings were not entirely uncommon.

The gangland scenario in Galveston was not enough to entice Sam and Rose out of their barbershop, as they were seekers of a certain financial opportunity that was not offered by the gangs until a national movement to suppress vice ironically made it more lucrative. The purpose of Prohibition was to reduce crime, improve the social fabric of communities, create a healthier and more hygienic population and decrease the financial burden of prisons on the taxpayers. It did none of these things because those goals were all dependent on getting people to stop drinking, which they did not. In fact, alcohol consumption and the prison population increased during Prohibition. Prohibitionists assumed that the money previously spent on alcohol would be diverted to more practical investments like life insurance and education, but per capita spending on alcohol only increased. Furthermore, since alcohol was illegal, neither the production nor the distribution of it could be regulated.[54]

Moonshiners became increasingly creative with their ingredients, and the alcohol by volume percentages spiked dramatically. Discretion was the key to distribution, so smugglers demanded the highest potency possible to minimize the number of cases and maximize profits on each one. This phenomenon was named the Iron Law of Prohibition, and it maintained that the more severe the law enforcement, the more potent the prohibited product. An article published by the *Galveston Daily News* in 1919 attested to this theory. It reported that a state inspection of 107 samples of illicit liquor taken from around Galveston revealed alcohol levels as high as 10.0 percent.[55] For context, the average beer was around 3.0 percent at the time, and the Volstead Act, enacted to allow for the enforcement of the Eighteenth Amendment, defined the limit for legally permitted alcohol as 0.5 percent.

Lack of regulation also meant an opaque production process, which often included harmful and sometimes lethal additives. Even though distillers discovered a safer alternative in corn sugar, the death rate from poisoned spirits was catastrophically high across the country, increasing 300 percent between 1920 and 1925. Another shortcoming was a complete inability to control the locations of bars, taverns and saloons. These required prominent real estate, but speakeasies could be small and hidden, tucked away in upper floors and back alleys. Local zoning laws were nonexistent, which meant that where cities previously had the authority to prohibit establishments from opening near schools, churches or civic centers, they now had no such jurisdiction. Rochester, New York, recorded twice as many speakeasies during Prohibition as it had saloons prior, and cities all over the nation were in a similar state.[56]

The spiked increase in demand for alcohol was fueled by three main groups. The ban on alcohol made it more intriguing to rebellious teenagers, and the exorbitant profits for smugglers meant that nondrinkers were actively recruited and converted. But it was the third group that cemented Galveston's early and extended reign over Gulf Coast smuggling and moonshining operations: old-stock Americans and recent immigrants who refused to be told they could not drink.[57] A kaleidoscopic demographic consisting largely of Italians, Germans and Irish created a deep-seated culture of opposition to prohibition in Galveston.[58] This demand for and acceptance of vice lasted long after the Eighteenth Amendment was repealed, carrying over to other illicit enterprises. Luckily, Galveston's two gangs were always looking for new opportunities, and they were more than happy to provide the supply.

Not foreseeing the disastrous effects of Prohibition, Texas went dry in April 1918 as a show of support for the proposed constitutional amendment. By the time it passed, the rumrunning, bootlegging and moonshining Texans already had a head start on the rest of the country. Johnny Jack, George, Dutch and Ollie were quick to add all three specialties to their résumés, and the island's direct access to the Gulf made it a magnet for low-level thugs looking to get in on the action. Johnny Jack took a wandering grifter named Francisco Raffele Nitti, known in Galveston as Frank Noonis, as an associate. The pair had been introduced in 1917 when Noonis was a small-time crook who sold watches and engaged in various petty criminal activities, but as soon as Prohibition hit and Johnny was in business, Frank cashed in on their friendship. Unfortunately, the price Johnny Jack paid for employing his pal was $24,000 when Noonis took off for Chicago with their shared profits. He changed his name and likely used the money to bankroll Al Capone, quickly working his way up the Windy City syndicate.[59] As Capone's executioner, he made a name for himself as Frank "The Enforcer" Nitti, but his debt to Galveston had yet to be paid.

Dutch and Ollie, on the other hand, made a much better decision than their downtown counterparts. They had taken a liking to the barbershop duet of Sam and Rose Maceo. Savvy Sam, with his million-dollar smile and the etiquette of a foreign aristocrat, was effortlessly diplomatic and had impeccable taste. His intelligence came in the form of an intense imagination and far-reaching vision coupled with a keen eye for beauty and a heart for service. Beside him was reticent Rose, the enigma who preferred to observe rather than to speak and whose silence was regularly mistaken for brooding. He was a human calculator, meticulous and precise, but in the shadows of his exacting mind would forever be the memories of unspeakable loss. To those he loved he was generous and kind, but to strangers he was cold and withdrawn. It was this public countenance, not his true self, that shored up his eventual reputation as the fierce enforcer.

At first, Sam and Rose were simply trying to round up business for the Beach Gang by providing samples of their Dago Red wine to barbershop customers, but soon, their patrons were smuggling out whole bottles, reportedly in hollowed-out loaves of French bread. Then, as fate would have it, the authorities fingered one of the Beach Gang's shipments, and Voight needed a place to stash it until the cops had moved on to another lead. The Maceo domicile was a raised beach cottage with ample space underneath for the storage of his fifteen hundred cases of hooch. For their services, Dutch offered Sam and Rose one dollar per case. In comparison, one haircut netted them twenty-five cents. A few days later, Voight came to retrieve the cache of liquor, but Rose declined the payment, asking instead that it be considered an investment in their next shipment.[60] Voight paused and looked carefully at Rose, a small smile twitching at the corners of his mouth. Then he reached out to shake his hand—he knew a businessman when he saw one.[61]

4

DOWN THE HATCH

Despite an overwhelming fear of being deported, Sam and Rose dove headfirst into the unique but risky opportunity that had presented itself.[62] They were officially in the bootlegging business, but they were not grifters or drifters looking to make a few bucks. They were investors, proprietors and visionaries, and they simply needed capital. Business loans were not readily available for men like the Maceos, and ironically, only after they became bootleggers could they walk into a bank and get a $100,000 loan on a signature.[63]

In theory, rumrunning was simple. Foreign ships laden with liquor would journey across the Gulf of Mexico from Cuba, Jamaica, the Bahamas or Honduras and anchor just over three miles from the Galveston shore, where U.S. jurisdiction ended and international waters began. Shrouded by darkness, or sometimes illuminated by the rare light of a smuggler's moon, men loaded into powerboats, fishing boats, motorized skiffs, flat-bottomed luggers or even rowboats and set off over the waves to rendezvous with their cargo. Wrapped in burlap sacks[64] and bundled in pairs, cases of the coveted nectar were hoisted over the side of the ship and lowered by a rope, with the sound of wood creaking and glass clinking the whole way down. The ship's captain would be paid with untraceable U.S. dollars, so it was an advantageous undertaking for both sides.

Risk factors into price, however, and a ship's haul was not nearly as much as that of the men slinking silently back to the beach in skiffs and motorboats. An average shipment was two thousand to three thousand cases, sometimes containing as many as twenty thousand, and this was not the "shook-up corn stuff" but brand-name liquors like Johnny Walker Black Label, Haig & Haig and Mumm's Extra Dry Champagne. Depending on who was doing the math, profit margins per case ranged from $4 to $125, but on average, the bootleggers would triple their investments, raking in anywhere from $10,00 to $300,000 per shipment.[65] That is, if they made it to shore. The pursuit of customs and the coast guard ended in capture and even water-borne gunplay more often than it did in escape. One enterprising pair who had been spotted by law enforcement decided to sink their haul and come back for it later, but the early morning beachcombers beat them to it when most of the bottles washed onto shore the next day.[66] Sometimes law enforcement would hide in the dunes and open fire as soon as the shipments hit the sand.[67]

The ideal scenario was to make it to the coastline unnoticed, and when they did, a group of anxious men would be waiting for them. At the first glimpse of their approaching comrades, the men would wade out into waist-deep water to beach the boat, retrieve the cases and lug them onto dry land. The liquor was then loaded onto trucks that barreled over the sand and dirt roads of the island's west end and to their destination. If they were not being delivered directly to a purchaser, the cases would sometimes be stored in remote hiding spots. The Beach Gang secreted its cases in a thicket of dunes and brush on the southwest corner of Sixty-First Street and Avenue S, across from the future location of the Maceo's Hollywood Dinner Club, and the Downtown Gang used the desolate beaches of San Luis Pass on the island's far western tip.[68] But these were not the only locations where they kept their cargo. Booze was stashed all over the city. Both gangs took advantage of the large number of pier-and-beam homes on the island that had plenty of room underneath for hundreds of cases and lattice around the bottom of the house for coverage. The liquor would sometimes be trucked to Houston and sometimes only as far as the Galveston railyard, where it was stowed away on trains headed to the Midwest.[69] Of course, it was not always that easy.

The potential for interference of origin ships increased substantially after the United States suggested to Great Britain that they each be allowed to examine the other's seagoing vessels past the three-mile limit of search and seizure and as far as twelve miles from shore. Not coincidentally, most of the ships smuggling booze were British. Long before the agreement was ever made official, U.S. Customs took the liberty of proceeding as if it was. Crews countered by installing fake smokestacks and plying up floor planks to create concealed compartments. Cases were stored in the engine room inside a tank labeled as lubricating oil, or five-gallon tin cans were cut open, filled with bottles and resealed. A 1923 bust uncovered several cases hidden within a lathe in the ship's machine shop and even more submerged in fifteen feet of water in the forepeak, the storage tank located in the extreme forward and lower portion of a ship.[70]

Regarding the other half of the transaction, opinions vary on the success of Galveston rumrunners. On one hand, Galveston did not garner nearly as much attention for smuggling as other ports like Boston, Florida, New York and the Virginia Capes. This is attributed to the fact that the bootleggers in Galveston were not (yet) as organized as their counterparts, nor were their criminal activities as vast or diverse. Local Prohibition officers are also given credit for having stymied the illegal imports, and the arrests and seizures reported in the 1920s are numerous.[71] On the other hand, several tales allude to the relative success of the operations in Galveston.

The island was lauded as the biggest hub of bootleg liquor on the Gulf Coast and was known to be a major supplier of outfits all over the Midwest and Southwest.[72] Both the Downtown Gang and the Beach Gang reportedly sold to Al Capone in Chicago at various times throughout Prohibition.[73] Johnny Jack Nounes and George Musey were both designated as the King of the Gulf Rumrunners at different points in their careers,[74] although knowing their braggadocious personalities, those may have been self-proclamations. Nounes was certainly known to spend most of his time walking the line between bravery and folly, and his rumrunning days were no exception. He had a fleet of wide, flat-bottomed boats that would bring his illegal cargo right in through the harbor and unload on the commercial docks. His prized possession was a speedboat named *Cherokee* that was almost uncatchable.[75]

Near the end of his life, Little Sammie Maceo told of unloading a shipment on the jetties a mere two hundred yards from an anchored coast guard vessel. "We didn't make any noise at all. There was no talking and no cigarette smoking. We'd take the liquor out, pass it along easily from man to man, and walk it into the truck. Then the truck would take off."[76] The Maceos also bested the coast guard by employing the alternative services of a local prostitute who was a regular entertainer of a certain higher-up. During their trysts, she gleaned information under the guise of being interested in the details of his work, such as how long he would be at sea, where they planned to patrol and any other insider information she could get him to dish.[77] Another triumphant story begins one December when a severe shortage left the whole state high and dry for an unknown reason. Maybe law enforcement had won a substantial victory, but regardless of the cause, deprived Texans were saved when the Maceos and the Beach Gang made like Santa Claus with a shipment of Christmas spirits that took more than a week to unload and saturated the county for months.[78]

The combined forces of the coast guard, the customs service and federal Prohibition agents were not without their own notable conquests, however. The coast guard set up a lookout on the top floors of the Buccaneer Hotel on the Seawall at Twenty-Third Street, and on three different occasions, they caught the *Cherokee*. Nounes and his ship were captured on March 11, 1922, with 350 cases of booze and then again in January 1924, while the speedboat was being unloaded on the west end. Both times, the *Cherokee* was seized, and both times, Johnny Jack bought it back at auction and put it back to work. Finally, on June 7, 1924, it was caught again while trying to slink past the south jetty and into the Gulf.[79] This time, customs agent Alvia "Al" Scharff made sure that customs was the one with the high bid at auction, and henceforth, the *Cherokee* became the pursuer.[80]

Three of the most active mother ships in the Gulf were the *Island Home*, the *Panama* and the *Muriel E. Winters*, all of which would often linger close to Galveston in international waters and act as floating warehouses until all of their cargo could be unloaded. This lively trio was also often on the receiving end of attention from Prohibition enforcement. In May 1924, the *Panama* was caught by a coast guard cutter named *Comanche*; aboard were 1,972 half cases and 100 full cases of liquor. *Muriel E. Winters* was busted with 9,552 bottles of whiskey at one point, and twelve crewmen were indicted for conspiracy to bring alcohol into U.S. waters. The American embassy in Havana tipped off authorities to the intentions of *Island Home* in 1923. It was seized on November 23, and its 1,709 burlap bags were stored in the customs appraiser's warehouse at Twenty-First and Water Streets (Avenue A, present-day Harborside Drive). These busts alone were calculated to have set the rumrunners back more than $1 million.[81]

Confiscations from the smaller boats used to ferry the liquor from the Gulf to the beach were just as plentiful. The Downtown Gang regularly borrowed a boat from one Tom Lena, but the *Lena* was captured in 1924 with 484 cases of Canadian Club whiskey, Bacardi rum and wine. A vessel named the *Rosalie M.* was caught later that year with 100 cases of Canadian Club, 25 cases of Bacardi and 25 cases of champagne, a stash with an estimated value of $10,000. By 1925, assistant customs collector Sam T. Zinn declared that "Rum Row" in Galveston was now nonexistent and that most of the liquor making its way to the island was coming via truck from New Orleans, but his optimism was negated by sustained efforts in the Gulf. In November 1926, seventeen representatives from the coast guard, customs and federal

Prohibition agencies held a conference that resulted in a restructuring of their strategy, and illegal liquor seizures continued in Galveston waters. In the late 1920s, the *Elizabeth* was corralled in Campbell's Bayou with 750 cases of liquor, and the *Emmy* registered 400 sacks of whiskey and 180 cases of raw alcohol, which rang up a total retail price of more than $30,000.[82]

Even if the shipments did make it to dry land, they were not always guaranteed safe passage. Both the Beach Gang and the Downtown Gang were wise to the fact that it was much easier to hijack a truck than it was to unload crates in the middle of the ocean, and each gang took turns victimizing the other. Trucks were even hijacked by regular residents looking to make a quick buck, but the threat of retribution was swift, and the trucks were usually returned, albeit sometimes missing the cargo. Later into the 1920s, when rumrunning on Galveston beaches was stymied and the Beach Gang began to funnel its shipments over land through Louisiana, George Musey of the Downtown Gang is thought to have used his New Orleans connections to frequently ambush their drivers and steal the truck's freight.[83]

Historically, the drama of rumrunning in Galveston has taken precedence and has likewise overshadowed the enormous amount of moonshining that was taking place in the city during Prohibition. Besides individual endeavors into bathtub gin and home-brewed beer, mass production for commercial use was rampant. The total output and monetary gains of moonshine are not traceable, but they can be deduced from the outrageous volume of bootleg brew that was discovered and destroyed, an amount significantly less than what was sold and consumed. In May 1923, six stills, ten gallons of raw whiskey and one thousand gallons of mash were located and demolished.[84] The very next month, a raid uncovered a fifty-gallon still and seized twenty-seven gallons of liquor, five barrels of mash and miscellaneous paraphernalia. The month after that, a smaller storehouse was discovered in town on Avenue P ½, and a search produced a one-hundred-gallon still, four barrels of mash and some whiskey. The following November, four small stills and twenty-five barrels of mash were confiscated from a house at Sixteenth Street and Avenue N.[85]

Starting in the mid-1920s, the stills and the liquor seizures became larger and larger, undoubtedly connected to a couple of popular restaurants and nightclubs that were opened. In 1924, local Prohibition agents seized their largest take yet when they were alerted to a massive operation in a house on the west side of town near Offatts Bayou. The makeshift distillery held two 75-gallon stills and one 36-gallon still, accompanied by 6,300 gallons of mash and 60 gallons of whiskey. A June 1926 raid exposed a 300-gallon still,

900 gallons of mash, 60 gallons of whiskey, 30 gallons of beer mash, 165 bottles of beer and another ten cases of empty bottles waiting to be filled. The largest still yet recovered was a 500-gallon brewer discovered on the west end in November 1928, but it was surpassed the following month when another one the same size was discovered along with 500 gallons of mash.[86]

The steadily increasing quantities of liquor being produced in Galveston were matched by an escalating number of soft drink or cold drink stands on the island, most of which were merely false fronts for the sale of liquor. This assumption matches the numerical evidence: Galveston had zero soft drink establishments in 1916 but listed seventy different soda stands in 1919, the year Prohibition was made official. Furthermore, the *Galveston Daily News* regularly published the names of those arrested on conspiracy liquor charges, and a substantial number of them were owners of cold drink stands. After reaching their peak in 1923, when city directories named more than one hundred of these businesses, the numbers steadily decreased throughout the remainder of the decade. In 1925, the number fell to seventy-four, then decreased to fifty-five the following year and bottomed out at twenty-four in 1934 after Prohibition was repealed.[87] The Maceos made the first investment of their bootlegging bucks in 1921 with the opening of one of these cold drink establishments, for which Sam was the face of the operation and Rose was the brains behind it. This initial business template foreshadowed their future, but the venue itself was a minor steppingstone. A vision and determination as fierce as theirs would soon be seeking endeavors far more grandiose than a soda stand.

5

THE MACEO MAGIC

The Beach and Downtown Gangs were content with the spoils of rumrunning and were happy to continue their charming anarchist antics, but the Maceos were on a different trajectory. Rather than being rebels for the sake of being rebellious, the Maceos were simply businessmen content to operate outside of legal technicalities. Sam and Rose used the financial impetus from bootlegging as the foundation of an empire, but the construction of it was slow, precise and deliberate. Sam was a born entertainer with endless creativity, while Rose was strategic with a perspicacious mind, and together, they held the winning combination of imagination and implementation. Over the next thirty years, the Maceo brothers displayed a remarkable resilience coupled with a cunning business acumen. They learned from their mistakes and shared in their successes.

Although vastly different in form and personality, Sam and Rose had each developed an earnest love for Galveston in their relatively brief island residency, and their mutual knowledge of poverty and hardship produced a genuine benevolence within them. From the beginning, Sam and Rose's entrepreneurial efforts were inspired by more than personal gratification. Revealing a deep affection for the city and its people, they established the Galveston Beach Association in 1920 and hired William Roe to promote the island as a resort destination.[88] Inspired initially by the island's potential—tropical weather, gorgeous cityscape and a seawall of wonder—the brothers instinctively knew that the success of their illicit endeavors would be contingent upon Galveston's legitimate reputation. Their willingness to invest in this manner from the outset illustrated a confidence in the future of their new island home that was repaid by residents with a sustained faith in their leadership.

William Roe's brilliant marketing abilities created the annual Aquatic Day, an official kick-off weekend to the summer season, which was anchored by the Bathing Girl Revue. The goal of Aquatic Day was not only to draw people to the island but also to elevate the standing of Seawall Boulevard and announce Galveston as a dignified resort city. Roe was aware that a fashionable city needed fashion itself, and for this reason, the Bathing Girl Revue was originally created as a costume contest aimed at infusing Seawall culture with couture.[89] The city estimated that twenty thousand people attended the inaugural event on May 23, 1920, and one local newspaper described it as a "solid mass of humanity" that stretched for miles, blanketed every fishing pier and spilled off the sidewalk into the street.[90] The crowds only got larger as the event continued to grow and evolve over the years. The name was changed to the more whimsical "Splash Day," and in 1926, Roe rebranded the revue as the International Pageant of Pulchritude and invited contestants from all over the world. After competing in three rounds of sportswear, swimwear and evening wear, the winner was dubbed Beauty Queen of the Universe. The format developed by Roe's Galveston pageant was later adopted and made world-famous by the Miss Universe contest.

Across the boulevard on the beachside, and opposite the stately Galvez Hotel built in 1911, Sam and Rose graduated from soda stand operators to real deal restaurateurs around 1923 when they purchased their first piece of Galveston real estate. The property was located over the water at Twenty-First Street and had previously been a fishing pier, an early pleasure pier and the Original Mexican Restaurant. Its first public mention came on August 29, 1924, when the Galveston Chamber of Commerce held a dinner for more than fifty of its new members, hosted by another new member, Sam Maceo. The paper referred to the chamber's milieu as simply, "The restaurant across the street from the Galvez," but Sam's debut to polite Galveston society was a smashing success and portended his eventual status as the ultimate host. Ollie Quinn had been more than a business partner in the years leading up to this night; he had been a mentor to Sam Maceo, who paid close attention to Quinn's deft ability to assuage the shortcomings of his private dealings with a sincere and generous public reputation. In addition to his affable demeanor, splendid cuisine

Bathing Girl Revue, 1930. *Rosenberg Library.*

and smuggled spirits, Sam presented musical numbers in between each course that displayed talents from Houston, New Orleans and Galveston. At the close of the evening, Sam announced that beginning September 15 the restaurant was to undergo an extensive remodel that was designed to resemble a famous café in downtown New York City.[91]

The Chop Suey Café opened on New Year's Eve 1925 to a capacity house that was so smitten with the elegance that attendees lingered until dawn. Billed as a "high class cabaret," the Chop Suey was yet another contribution to the Maceos' vision of a glamorous, elite island resort culture. The restaurant featured delicate lattice work interlaced with Chinese wisteria, a raised platform for the orchestra and tables arranged neatly around the perimeter of a large dance floor. The interior was illuminated by a dramatic lighting scheme that included a dimly lit dining room and a dance floor punctuated by a spotlight for the performers. Behind the scenes, Chop Suey's kitchen was outfitted with the most modern of appliances and culinary effects. Sam spoke with enthusiasm to the press, declaring that his desire was to make islanders proud by providing Galveston with a sophisticated, high-class cabaret.[92]

Within a few short months, Chop Suey was regaled as one of the most popular establishments on the island and had achieved something extremely rare for an entertainment venue in Galveston: year-round patronage. In fact, most other Seawall businesses were known to close for the duration of the winter, but Sam and Rose were confident that if given the right motivation, people's interest in visiting the island would be impervious to the seasons.

7 Eleventh Annual Bathing Girl Revue. August 2,3,4,5,6, 1930. Maurer, Copyright, 1930.

They trademarked their restaurant by providing an experience, not simply a meal, even though the cuisine was top-notch. The house specialty was chop suey itself, delightfully garnished with live entertainment from both visiting artists and the restaurant's resident performers George McQueen's Chop Suey Fun Makers.[93]

Over on the north side of the island, things were not going quite as well for one of the leaders of the Downtown Gang. The impeccable fashion sense of Johnny Jack Nounes branded him the "Beau Brummel of Galveston," and his generosity earned him the title "Robin Hood of the Gulf," but his mettlesome personality and tales of $40,000 parties in New York City made him an easy target. On January 3, 1924, his reputation caught up with him when he was captured on the west end of the island brazenly unloading cargo from the *Cherokee* in broad daylight.[94] In a tale that has immortalized Johnny Jack's bravado, the sitting judge on his case initially fined him $5,000.

"Hell judge, I've got that much right here in my right-hand pocket!" Nounes boasted.

"Then reach in your left-hand pocket," the judge responded, "and see if you can find two years in the penitentiary."[95]

Mere months later, Johnny Jack was out on appeal when he was arrested again in connection with seizures of the *Betty Pat* and the *Rosalie M.*[96] Four others were charged along with him in what the local papers referred to as the Galveston Rum War. On April 9, 1925, at 4:00 p.m., the judge called the jury to the courtroom. The jurors had been deadlocked for twenty-four hours at an eleven to one vote in the verdict of Nounes and Company's most recent charges. Not knowing whether the stand-alone vote was for acquittal or conviction, both legal teams agreed to let the verdict of the eleven

Bathing Girl Revue, 1932. *Rosenberg Library.*

The Chop Suey Cafe, Opposite Hotel Galvez, Galveston, Texas.

Postcard depicting the Chop Suey Café. *Rosenberg Library.*

represent the whole. The verdict was "not guilty," and all five men were released.[97] Robin Hood's luck ran out two months later, however, when the circuit court of appeals in New Orleans upheld the two-year prison sentence from his 1924 trial in Galveston.[98] In Johnny Jack's absence, George Musey assumed sole leadership of the Downtown Gang and managed to maintain a low profile for a couple of years despite an escalating rivalry with newly appointed customs officer Al Scharff.

On Scharff's first day of work in 1924, he sought out an infamous Houston hijacker named Mitch Frankovich who was reported to have successfully hijacked shipments from both the Beach and Downtown Gangs. The day that Scharff found him, Frankovich was nursing wounds from a recent beating at the hands of Johnny Jack and was fearful that similar punishments from his other victims were inevitable. These were the perfect conditions for Scharff to suggest a deal. He offered Frankovich protection, dropped several charges he was facing and promised future leniency. In return, Frankovich agreed to help Scharff in his pursuit of other Galveston rumrunners and to use his hijacking skills to seize shipments, becoming the first of many criminals turned informants who Scharff would use in the rum wars.[99]

Back in Beach Gang territory, the success of Sam and Rose's Chop Suey Café had commanded the full attention of Dutch and Ollie, who were seeking to expand their holdings to a property on Sixty-First Street. Along that two-lane road on the western outskirts of town, Voight and Quinn, along with a Russian immigrant named Jake Friedman, had purchased a lot on the northwest corner of Stewart Road, where they intended to build a nightclub and gambling house. Friedman was a walking eccentricity. Not an inch over five feet tall, with an affinity for western wear, his fragrance of choice was a women's perfume called White Shoulders.[100] When Friedman opted for a Houston venture and decided to sell his interest in the Galveston project, Sam and Rose were the likely choice to take his place. Upon accepting the invitation, the two Maceos masterminded a concept that combined the Beach Gang's small-scale gambling forays with their effortless panache and unrivaled showmanship.

The Hollywood Dinner Club was designed by local Galveston architect R. Rapp to meet precise specifications that included gambling dens and a main floor that could seat five hundred guests. The property sprawled across an entire city block and was crowned with Rapp's Spanish Colonial Revival building that featured a traditional barrel-tiled, mission-style roof and floor-to-ceiling windows. The building perimeter was layered with immaculate landscaping and a circular drive. An eight-foot-tall iron fence encompassed

Above: The Hollywood Dinner Club was built in 1926 on the corner of Sixty-First Street and Stewart Road. *Rosenberg Library*.

Left: Advertisement for Hollywood Dinner Club. Galveston Monthly *magazine*.

the entire lot, interrupted only by a twenty-six-foot-wide set of gates that were handmade by a local ironworker named Albert Voigt for the staggering sum of $2,500 (nearly $40,000 today).

Inside, the ceiling dripped with the crystals of massive chandeliers that flickered their light down onto gleaming, caramel-colored hardwood floors. Crisp linens and polished silver were laid on the tables with military-like precision by waiters who were rigorously and personally trained by Sam Maceo. Long before restaurants made it a common requirement of employment, Sam Maceo's staff learned about the food they were serving, but more importantly, they learned how to be gentlemen. They were schooled in the art of superb service, as Sam insisted that his guests should never even have to light their own cigarettes.[101] The club was one of the first in the nation to be air conditioned, and Sam instructed his staff to keep the room at sixty-nine degrees to keep guests deliciously cool. So cool that they could not feel the liquor. So cool that they could gamble more and care less. The back rooms, accessible via small doors at the rear of the dining room, housed thirty craps tables, no fewer than three blackjack tables, several roulette wheels and endless slot machines.[102] Before the Hollywood, prior to the Maceos, no one had ever combined gourmet food, high-end gambling, impeccable service and elite entertainers all under one roof, but Sam's sense of the spectacular was not limited to the floor of the club.

He and William Roe developed an ingenious marketing strategy for the opening season that centered on securing a slate of world-class entertainment for the entire summer, including their grand opener, the "big-time talent" of Guy Lombardo and his Royal Canadians, who were often billed as "the sweetest music this side of heaven." Lombardo performed on opening night and drew nearly twenty thousand people to the Hollywood over the next three weeks during his temporary residency. Riding the prestige of their booked entertainers, who were not always famous but were always personally handpicked by Sam's exquisite taste, Maceo and Roe were able to convince radio station KFUL to broadcast live from the club. This was one of the first remote broadcasts in the nation. The contract stipulated that KFUL would air from the Hollywood Dinner Club from 9:00 p.m. to midnight three nights a week for three months.[103]

On June 5, 1926, the airways ignited with the sounds of Hollywood glamour as the dinner club opened its doors for the first time, revealing a swank and swagger that rivaled London's famous Kit Kat Club.[104] The colorful broadcast described the scene in detail, and everyone listening felt like they were part of the Hollywood's opening night. In 1926, a working-class man's wages were approximately $1.00 per day, and a movie ticket was $0.35. An average tab at Hollywood Dinner Club totaled $15.00, which included a $1.65 cover charge but not any wagers made in the back rooms. The radio broadcasts bridged the gap and transmitted a sense of ownership, cultivating a fondness for the Hollywood and the Maceos in people who never stepped one foot inside the club.

The first summer season closed on September 1, 1926, and the final KFUL broadcast featured George McQueen, who went on to become a smashing success in Chicago and who Sam considered a protégé because his first professional gig was at the Chop Suey.[105] Back-to-back variety programs titled "School Days" and "The Battle of Flowers" bookended the season with nonstop entertainment and spectacle that officially installed Sam

Above: Casino chips from the Hollywood Dinner Club. *Anonymous private collection.*

Left: Receipt for Hollywood Dinner Club, date May 11, 1927. Galveston Monthly *magazine.*

Maceo as the king of Galveston nightlife.[106] Wearing a tailored tuxedo with a white carnation slipped into the lapel, Sam's presence was as much of a draw as any entertainer he hired. The Hollywood Dinner Club personified his smooth, sophisticated style, which would have been ostentatious if it were not so unaffected and genuine. He planned a complete redecoration of the club's interior for the winter season opening, which was postponed until November 16 to allow for its completion.[107] He also needed the additional time to stage the opening production, which included six different sets of live performances, a display the *Galveston Daily News* described as "a gala atmosphere, unsurpassed by that of any previous occasion."[108]

Unfortunately, the Hollywood was deposed as Galveston's reigning goddess of vice on May 11, 1927, shortly after the opening of its second summer season.[109] Temporary injunctions were filed against the club for gaming violations and were approved by county judge Charles G. Dibrell of the Fifty-Sixth District Court on July 6. When undercover operatives infiltrated the club one month later and found that the injunction had been ignored and gambling continued, Texas state attorney general Claude Pollard launched a two-sided attack against Sam Maceo. First, his office filed *quo warranto* proceedings that petitioned the courts to revoke the Hollywood's charter, and then he charged Sam with contempt of court for violating the temporary injunction. These actions made guests of the

Stir sticks from the Hollywood and Turf that name Sam Maceo as the manager. *Anonymous private collection.*

club apprehensive, and attendance dropped as the posh ambiance was overshadowed by fear of the "annoyance and humiliation" that would accompany a spontaneous visit from law enforcement. Sam addressed the issue with the press, saying, "I have tried to conduct the Hollywood Club on a plane that would reflect credit upon Galveston and to provide a place of amusement that the best people in the community would not be ashamed to patronise [*sic*]. That I have succeeded seems to be borne out by the fact I have received hundreds of complaints on the place and the manner in which it was operated by those prominent in the social, business, and political life of Texas."[110]

Sam did not immediately divine the lesson inherent in his statement, but he did carry on undeterred. After the summer of 1927, the Hollywood was only open sporadically, usually for private parties that were seldom advertised or announced. Sam and Rose turned their attention back to their Seawall property. They partnered with Voight to remodel the Chop Suey in 1928. It was renamed the Grotto, and in addition to a new thematic interior, the build-out was restructured to allow for gambling rooms. Mere months after the grand reopening, at 1:00 a.m. on July 3, 1928, Sheriff R.E. Kirk served injunctions to Dutch Voight at the Grotto and to the owner of another alleged gambling house. He also had injunctions for three other owner/operators who he was not able to locate. Sam Maceo and George Musey were on that list.[111] The next year brought another wave of gambling charges, and Sam was on the hook again, joined this time by Ollie Quinn and his DeLuxe Club. In November 1929, they both pleaded guilty to four counts of "keeping a room for the purpose of being used as a place to gamble" and paid fines of $500 for each count.[112] Exasperated, Sam closed the Grotto indefinitely, and it was henceforth rented out to Galveston businessman Louie Morris.[113] Sam had learned his first lesson the hard way: concocting the most magnificent nightlife concept ever created was not enough—he had to use his talents outside the club as well as inside. In the moment of this realization, Sam Maceo went from debonair nightclub manager to full-fledged diplomat.

Although historians have long speculated that the Maceos must have employed bribery as a means of insulating their decades-long empire, no official records, statements or criminal charges of extortion exist to corroborate those accusations. Instead, Sam and Rose deftly maneuvered around the system and built their credibility by making the most of circumstances as they arose.

Their first opportunity came as a result of Musey's ever-growing hatred of Al Scharff. After violently murdering at least one of Scharff's informants, the customs officer himself became the bullseye. Musey recruited a couple of Chicago henchmen for his first attempt. They stopped for a drink in a local bar before they headed out to find Scharff. The bar they chose was frequented by one of the Maceo's bodyguards, who befriended the out-of-towners and learned their intention. Sam was notified and arrived at the bar promptly to explain to his new Chicago pals that "one Al Scharff was less trouble than the 50 agents that would replace him if he were murdered."[114] He leaned in and lowered his voice, but the words did not need to be spoken. If anyone else had come in his stead, the outcome surely would have been different. Call it a threat, or call it diplomacy, the pair quickly left the bar and headed back north. Sam had not only saved Scharff's life but also the lives of his assassins, demonstrating to both sides a desire for peace and nonviolence whenever possible.

A couple of months later, Musey tried once more and this time brought in two executioners from Kentucky. Upon their arrival, the Maceos arranged for some of their men to guard Scharff's family, house and vehicle, while others found the killers and promptly escorted them out of town. Meanwhile, Scharff's family and other customs officers were in a panic because they had been searching all day for the customs agent who had somehow managed to wander off without anyone knowing where he went. That evening, he returned home completely unaware of all that had transpired and hastened to explain to his frantic wife that he had made a random decision to go to the picture show. He had fallen asleep and stayed in the theater for seven hours.[115] The Maceos had proven themselves protective and respectful of local law enforcement, and their ulterior motive did nothing to diminish the effect. But for added insurance, they hired Louis C. Dibrell, son of the county judge, and Emmet Magee, brother of county prosecutor Raymond Magee, as their attorneys.[116]

6

WE OWN DOWNTOWN

While Sam and Rose were working to solidify their standing in the community, the leaders of the two Galveston gangs were slowly losing their clout and succumbing to the cumulative effects of decades' worth of criminal activity and arrests. The Maceos are often assumed to have accelerated their upward mobility and eventual takeover of the Galveston underground by squeezing out their competition forcefully or with the use of threats, but the empirical history belies this notion, pointing instead to hardened criminals whose efforts had infuriated state and federal officials and compromised their ability to operate surreptitiously. Furthermore, the former leaders of the Beach and Downtown Gangs continued to run smaller-scale vice dens even after their crews had disbanded and the Maceos had taken center stage, and all but one of them lived peacefully in Galveston for the rest of their lives. Sam and Rose's leadership was far from tyrannical, and their laissez-faire attitude toward government was complemented and bolstered by a live-and-let-live policy toward their fellow residents and business owners. Their authority was never questioned, not because the Maceos ruled by fear, but because they continually demonstrated their commitment to the well-being of Galveston.

Ollie Quinn was the first to exhibit signs of a wavering fortitude when in 1928 he fatally shot a man named Ray Maledo in the middle of the day on the corner of Twenty-Fifth and Church Streets. The one eyewitness in the case, D.D. Alexander, testified during the inquest hearing that he was driving in downtown Galveston on the day of the shooting and saw Quinn standing outside on the sidewalk as he passed through the intersection of Twenty-First and Postoffice Streets. When Alexander pulled over to park his car, Quinn asked him if he would "take him around to see another fellow." When they reached Church and Twenty-Fifth, Maledo came up to the window of the car. Quinn stepped out and asked him about money that he was owed, and although they appeared at first to be making an arrangement for the debt to be repaid, Maledo suddenly shouted, "I won't pay it and I'll cut your—heart out." Maledo punched Quinn twice, and a shot was fired. Quinn immediately walked to the police station and surrendered to the chief of police, Pat Sullivan. He handed the chief his .44 and said, "I just shot a man, here's my gun." The judge returned a decision of death by gunshot with homicidal intent, to which Quinn pled self-defense, and he was released on a bond signed by Rose Maceo.[117]

No criminal trial proceedings for the incident were ever reported, but Quinn was nabbed again for running a gambling house in 1929, after which he disappeared from public eye, though the charges were dismissed.[118] He remained a successful businessman and respected resident of Galveston, owning a multitude of investments and participating in local organizations. Quinn sold his interests in the Hollywood Dinner Club to Dutch Voight but retained ownership of his club at 2017 Postoffice Street and changed the name to the more innocuous Deluxe Billiard Club. Across the street at 2024 Postoffice, he operated the Deluxe Novelty Company and the Home Plate Cigar Store, as well as The Pilot Bar at 413 Twenty-First Street and an apartment building on the corner of Forty-Fifth and Avenue O½. In 1938, he received notice for sponsoring and assisting the chamber of commerce when they decorated downtown Galveston for Christmas, and as a veteran of World War I, Quinn was an active member of the Veterans of Foreign Wars (VFW) and the American Legion.

On a Tuesday morning, August 23, 1949, Quinn left Galveston at 3:00 a.m. and headed in the direction of Dallas. Five hours later, while driving on Highway 75, fifty-six-year-old Ollie Quinn stepped on the gas and continued to accelerate toward a car traveling a few yards ahead of him in the same direction. Quinn did not reduce his speed as he approached the vehicle and rear-ended it going at least fifty-five miles per hour. The cars locked together, and the other driver was thrown into the backseat but managed to crawl back into the driver's seat, bringing the crashed caravan to a stop in a ditch. Quinn was killed instantly when the impact crushed the steering wheel against his chest.[119]

The saga that propelled George Musey and Johnny Jack Nounes to their ultimate fates began in June 1928, when they were both captured in Seabrook while unloading a shipment of booze from the *Lena* and the *Imperator*. The Downtown Gang had been trying to avoid the customs agents and coast guard by landing illegal cargo at points along the mainland coast. On May 12, 1929, Musey and Nounes were found guilty on seven counts of smuggling liquor into the United States.[120] At their sentencing trial on May 18, the judge lambasted them both, telling Nounes that he had "bothered me more than any person in my district." They were given three two-year sentences to be served concurrently, and five-year suspended sentences, which would be contingent upon good behavior. Musey was fined $5,000, but Nounes received a reduced fine of $500 after claiming that he was unable to pay the $5,000 as he had previously.[121] Again, they appealed their sentences. While out on bond and awaiting their new hearing, Musey was indicted on additional charges in the anti-liquor campaign, along with twenty-one other men.[122] Nounes was also facing two other federal hearings, one of which was his first and only acquittal.[123]

In January 1930, the appellate court denied Nounes and Musey's appeal, reinstated the sentence and instructed them to report to the county jail on February 28 to be transported to Atlanta Leavenworth Penitentiary.[124] Johnny Jack showed, but Musey did not. By ignoring his summons, Musey became a fugitive and forfeited his $10,000 bond, which made headlines as the largest forfeited bond on county record.[125] Seventeen months later, he was apprehended in his hometown of Lake Charles, Louisiana, with his old rival Dutch Voight, who had all but vanished since the closing of the Grotto. After being transported back to Galveston, Musey was held in a hotel room and denied any visitation while his paperwork was processed. The next morning, he was escorted to the county jail wearing a crisp blue button-down shirt with a striped necktie, auburn trousers, a pair of wingtip Oxfords and a gaudy gold wristwatch. He was allowed to see his family and gave a spirited interview to the press, smiling broadly and remarking how good it was to be back and that he had planned on giving himself up before he was captured. He also substantiated the rumor sparked by the identity of his companion. The incessant pursuit of both gangs had prompted the Beach and Downtown Gangs to gather at a secret combine where they formed an alliance and agreed to end the rivalry stoked by informing hijackers and customs men of one another's whereabouts. During their absence, Voight and Musey were operating as business partners; traveling between Canada, Central America, Louisiana and Galveston; and attempting to secure inventory. Their efforts led them directly into a trap set by Scharff's successor E.A. Gleason.[126]

The Maceos, meanwhile, had committed themselves to a low profile, temporarily abandoning the entertainment business and focusing on other investments. They formed the Gulf Vending Company, which rapidly gained prominence over Ollie Quinn's Modern Vending in providing every grocery, drugstore, bar, washeteria, restaurant and liquor store in Galveston with slot machines. Owners were not asked if they wanted the machines but were merely asked how many they wanted, but their profit share was a generous 50 percent. Most businesses depended on the income from their machines, while others made more off the slots than their storefronts.[127] The income from Gulf Vending sustained Sam and Rose while they endured the holdover, but they held fast to their vision of bringing state- and nationwide acclaim to the island.

On August 6, 1932, the Maceo family organized the Turf Athletic Club (TAC), the umbrella company under which all of their current and future gambling enterprises would operate. In later decades, tax records named Sam, Rose, Dutch Voight, Frank Maceo and D.D. Alexander as the original organizers of the TAC. Alexander was a "natty, blade-thin rambler" who is credited with bringing legalized horseracing to Galveston and inspiring Sam and Rose to the gambling trade.[128] In 1935, the founding structure was reorganized. Sam, Rose, Dutch Voight and Sam "Books" Serio—the TAC accountant who was a Maceo relation via Sam and Rose's maternal grandmother—each owned 20 percent, while Sam and Rose's cousins, brothers Vic C. and Frank Maceo, each owned 10 percent.[129] Three years later, Arthur J. Adams purchased 10 percent of Serio's share and remained a partner into the 1950s.

Gambling chip of Turf Athletic Club. *Anonymous private collection.*

Six days after the Turf was organized, the hurricane of 1932 struck the neighboring town of Freeport. Galveston was spared significant damage, but a large number of properties along the Seawall were severely battered by the high winds, one of which was the old Grotto. Repairs to the property were unavoidable, thus Sam and Rose thought it fitting that their first new endeavor under the TAC badge would include their reentrance into the world of entertainment.

Postcard advertising the opening of the Sui Jen. *Anonymous private collection.*

Calls flooded in, but the other end of the line always conveyed unfortunate news: The grand opening of the Sui Jen Café was completely booked and had been for weeks.[130] On Wednesday, November 2, 1932, less than three months after the hurricane, Sam debuted the Maceos' remarkable new venue to an "awed and admiring public." An illuminated dragon greeted guests at the doorway, the interior lights resembled Chinese lanterns and every minute detail was calculated to create an otherworldly experience. Additionally, the pier off the back of the restaurant had been extended two hundred feet. The name was chosen by William Roe, who had become one of Sam's most trusted advisors and was named manager of the Sui Jen. At the club's opening, Roe enlightened the curious crowd by revealing that the name was pronounced "swee ren" and that the inspiration for it came from an ancient Chinese philosopher who invented cooking and dancing. Shortly after this declaration, Galveston was visited by an assistant to the Chinese consul, Mr. King Tung Chon. Mr. Chon scoffed at Roe's designation, announcing that it was pronounced exactly how it was spelled and that it meant "crystal" in Chinese, and then continued his arrogant mockery by saying that cooking and dancing go as far back as recorded history.[131]

The fastidious William Roe disputed the consulate by returning to the Rosenberg Library, where he had researched countless volumes of Chinese

Left: An extremely rare casino chip from the Sui Jen. *Anonymous private collection.*

Below: Invitation to the opening of the Sui Jen in 1932. *Family collection.*

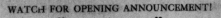

WATCH FOR OPENING ANNOUNCEMENT!

" "

on the Pleasure Pier—21st and Boulevard

The Hollywood Dinner Club management takes pride and pleasure in announcing the opening, within a few weeks, of a new and distinctive dine and dance club on the site formerly occupied by "The Grotto".

It will be renamed appropriate to the Oriental decorative motif to be employed and will be the last word in smart and exclusive resorts of its kind and character.

Watch daily newspapers for opening date.

Sam Maceo
Managing Director

1947, Sam Maceo, General Jimmie Doolittle, Mayor Herbert Cartwright.

To Our Patrons:

According to Chinese mythology, Sui Jen (pronounced "swee rin") as most authorities agree, lived many thousands of years ago and was the outstanding cultural hero of his time.

Sui Jen is credited with two major contributions to the welfare of mankind, cooking and dancing.

He invented the stick for "churning" fire. One historian has called him the Chinese Prometheus. After this came the invention of cooking, possibly in the way which Charles Lamb has so entertainingly described in his famous essay, "A Dissertation on Roast Pig."

Other arts of life logically followed in the wake of the culinary art, including that of dancing. This, we are told, first came into vogue not as an amusement but as an hygienic exercise.

Because we shall strive to offer our guests the best in Chinese cuisine and service, to furnish a setting and the kind of music that will enable you to enjoy dancing to the utmost and, further, because we hope to play host in the traditionally perfect manner of the true Oriental, we have chosen the name Sui Jen.

Respectfully yours,

Sam Maceo
Managing Director

SUI JEN

Menu

Opening Night
Wednesday, November 2, 1932

history in search of a name for his employer's restaurant that was both meaningful and phonetically distinctive. He located his original source, Gowen and Hall's *Outline History of China*, and presented it directly to the press. The book explored Chinese myths and legends, and Sui Jen was purported to be the Chinese counterpart to Greek mythology's Prometheus, the creator of fire.

"After this came the invention of cooking," Roe stated. "Other arts of life logically followed in the wake of the culinary art, including that of dancing… [which] came into vogue not as an amusement but as an [*sic*] hygienic exercise." Roe's source also stated that the hero's name was pronounced "swee ren." Successfully vindicated, Roe returned the book to the library, and the issue was closed.[132]

On the heels of Sui Jen's opening, Galveston was dealt a semisweet victory in April 1933 when the Texas House of Representatives and Senate introduced an amendment to the state constitution that would repeal Prohibition. Its ratification required approval from the voting populace, and it was placed on a special election ballot scheduled for August 26. On the evening of August 24, Congressman Joe Eagle of Houston addressed fifteen hundred Galveston voters at Menard Park at Twenty-Eighth and Seawall Streets, and he declared the Eighteenth Amendment a "monstrosity" and urged its repeal on the grounds that it violated three essential principles of government: personal liberty, local rights and state sovereignty. These violations were proven by another stark fact—Prohibition was a complete failure.[133]

"Before prohibition there were 667 breweries in the United States," Eagle said. "Last year I'll bet there were 10,000 in Houston alone." Hyperbole aside, he cited the sworn statements of federal Prohibition officials who testified that the amount of illegal alcohol seized in 1931 was already greater than the amount produced legally in the year before Prohibition had taken effect, even without the substantial hauls that had gone undiscovered and undocumented. He further maintained that the income derived from liquor was financing crime instead of generating tax revenue. In a more passionate appeal, he reminded the audience of the ideals of personal liberty upon which the United States was founded and its government organized:

There are two classes of law—natural and artificial. We all know instinctively that murder and robbery and certain other things, are wrong. But conscience doesn't tell me that it is wrong to smoke a cigarette, or take a chew of tobacco, or drink a glass of beer. Laws against such things are artificial and unnatural; juries won't convict, and judges won't sentence men for their violation….Let us see what personal liberty means. It means the right to come and go as you want; to have what religion you want; to enter whatever trade you want; and to eat and drink what you want.[134]

Eagle also discussed the right and responsibility of local and state governments to reflect the ideals of its specific constituencies, explaining that the founding fathers of the United States never desired a federal government that would regulate the intimate lives of Americans. Rather, they limited the federal government to hold only the powers necessary to facilitate the harmonious interaction of the states. In this vein, he praised Galveston, New Orleans and San Francisco as cities "which have kept their freedom and refused to surrender to the 18th Amendment….I have heard [others] refer to the free parts of the country as beds of iniquity. I have been able to reply to two of these men that these cities have their freedom, and that the other cities will follow." The crowd erupted in rapturous applause.[135] Two days later, Galveston County voters supported repeal with a thirteen-to-one majority. Three months after that, national Prohibition was repealed on November 29 when Utah became the thirty-sixth state to ratify the Eighteenth Amendment's removal.[136] The bootleggers, rumrunners and moonshiners were criminals no longer, but that also meant that they were stripped of their most lucrative business.

In February 1932, another round of sweeping charges had been brought against Dutch Voight, his imprisoned ally George Musey and nearly twenty other men in connection with the Lake Charles operation that remanded Musey.[137] On March 6, 1933, Dutch was arrested again and indicted on liquor charges with twenty-seven others,[138] but he remained out on bond until January 20, 1934, when his became one of the last Prohibition cases tried in federal court. The cases against the other men were dismissed, but Voight was penalized with a $5,000 fine. Customs officers claimed that he was a lieutenant of Musey's, but regardless of the semantics, Voight was reported to be a well-moneyed man with a net worth between $500,000 and $2 million.[139] While Voight had been wrangling with the courts, the Maceos' proprietary talents had cornered the underground markets, but he remained a close friend and business associate of theirs for the rest of his life. He held on to his minority ownership of the TAC, and his daughter Estelle Voight married Vincent Maceo, the son of Sam and Rose's cousin Frank. Over the next fifteen years, Dutch slowly sold off his TAC shares to Vincent, but his gangster days were never far behind him. Until his death in 1986, Voight kept firearms stashed all around his house—under couch cushions, behind the toilet—just in case.[140]

Johnny Jack wrote to a reporter from prison in 1930 asking for clippings of stories and pictures that had been printed during his incarceration and admitting that he liked to see his name in print.[141] Indeed, after his release, his criminal endeavors continued, as did his ability to make the local paper. The *Lena/Imperator* case of 1929 was still making headlines in 1931, first when Musey was caught and again when two other men charged in that case, George and Douglas Etie, were later tried for intimidating witnesses in Nounes's and Musey's trials.[142] Johnny Jack's next headline came in 1933, when he and another man were fined on an assault charge for pistol-whipping a man in Galveston after an "argument over nothing."[143] Around this time, Nounes drifted north to Houston and operated various businesses, including a liquor store at 4008 Main Street, where he also sold by the glass. Since liquor was only legally saleable by the bottle in Texas, and liquor by the drink was still illegal despite the repeal of Prohibition, Nounes managed to rack up another decade's worth of liquor charges.[144] In the late 1930s, he and his wife owned the Highway Inn on South Highway 8 in Houston. Once estimated to be a millionaire, Johnny Jack's later financial situation was brought to light when he was arrested on unspectacular robbery charges in 1940 for holding up a woman and relieving her of $1,500 in cash.[145]

Nounes then returned to Galveston where he owned and operated the Crystal Club at 2406 Market Street, formerly owned by George Musey and regularly visited by lawmen attempting to thwart his over-the-counter sale of alcohol. In a particularly busy year for Johnny Jack, liquor charges were filed against him in March 1943; a warrant for his arrest on a different matter was issued in August; and then on October 10, 1943, he went to trial for operating an open saloon, which resulted in a hung jury.[146] Johnny Jack Nounes finally began to make headlines of a different sort when he won the 1947 election for mayor of West Beach, but his legitimacy was short-lived when the victory was promptly followed by voter fraud allegations, of which a 1949 jury found him guilty.[147] One of his last and most humorous bouts with the law came in 1954 when Johnny Jack tied a barge to the Galveston causeway and operated it as a floating bait shop, bar and café. He was ordered by the state to remove the barge, and he readily complied by sailing it less than one mile to the east. The barge was now out of state territory and within Galveston city limits, but local law enforcement charged him for selling beer without a permit.[148] His clever trickery and malapert personality made him a notable island character for the remainder of his life, and he was once again elected to public office in 1960 as the mayor of Pirates Beach. His death in 1970, two months after his eightieth birthday, was mourned by all of Galveston.

George Musey circumvented an onslaught of charges in the late 1920s aside from his rumrunning debacles. An attempted murder case against him was dropped when the key witness failed to appear in court in June 1928.[149] Charges of both keeping and maintaining a pool hall and keeping and exhibiting slot machines were dismissed a few months later when the only witness for the state testified that he was unable to make certain identifications or to remember the dates and places regarding the accused.[150] Musey's eventual capture for the *Lena/Imperator* charges did nothing to stifle the confidence his "luck" had afforded him, and after serving less than four years of a six-and-a-half-year sentence, Musey was released in January 1934. He was eager to get back into business on the island. He worked alongside his brother Fred who was operating the Crystal Club on Market Street and ventured into the marble (pinball) machine racket. The machines themselves were legitimate, but coercion from the wrong end of a strong arm was usually responsible for their installation in various businesses that received a miniscule percentage of the profits. Musey was seeking to expand this venture by purchasing more marble machines and acquiring a new type of horseracing machine from Stanley and Ed Payne, coin machine agents from Houston. In an outing that combined both business and pleasure, Musey and the Payne brothers visited several bars in Galveston before stopping into the Alamo Club at Twenty-Fourth and Church Streets in the early morning hours of July 25, 1935.[151]

Prior to the Alamo, the three had wandered into the Silver Dollar on Postoffice Street where they ran into Julius "Frenchy" Etie. Musey asked him to accompany them to the Alamo for a late-night meal. The four men were seated at a table, conversing, drinking and waiting on their food when a man, identified by one witness in court as O.J. "Windy" Goss, walked in through the side door and asked Musey to follow him out into the alleyway because someone needed to talk to him. This was not a request Musey would have obliged to an unknown stranger. To the contrary, Goss had been with Musey and Dutch Voight in Lake Charles when they were arrested. When Goss himself was later arrested and charged with rumrunning and harboring a fugitive, he attested that he was at the same hotel as Musey and Voight, but he "did not know who they were." According to associates of Musey, Goss obtained employment with the Maceos upon returning to Galveston but had recently befriended George. They met for coffee almost daily, and the subsequent conversations often centered on Windy's disenchantment with his employer. He complained that they had cut his pay, so he quit, and although Musey never offered him employment, a considerable amount of trust must have been established for him to stand and follow a man to the side door of the Alamo.[152]

Musey had barely cleared the doorframe when a series of shots were fired so quickly that patrons of the restaurant initially mistook them as fireworks. Musey collapsed in the doorway, bleeding heavily from five gunshot wounds. Three of the bullets struck his neck, abdomen and right thigh, while two others lodged in his chest. The shooter fled on foot. Moments later, a police officer spotted Windy Goss running north toward the harbor on Twenty-Fourth Street and fired a warning shot in his direction. Goss stopped immediately, dropped a .38 caliber to the ground and explained to the officer as he was being put into the police wagon, "They tried to get me. They were looking for me all over the beach." Goss was later acquitted of the charges due to lack of both evidence and corroborative witnesses—Etie was able to identify Goss, but Ed Payne was not.[153] Ed Payne had instinctively followed Musey to the door after he was summoned, although Payne admitted in court that he was not expecting trouble and that he could not explain why he would follow a client to a private conversation. Payne reached Goss just as he fell and looked right at the shooter, but he testified that even though he had seen him, "if he was standing right there before me, I wouldn't recognize him." Apparently, his memory was interrupted when a dying George Musey looked up and said his last words. "Ed, they got me."[154]

As Musey was bleeding out and Goss was being handcuffed, Rose Maceo and his bodyguard Jim Crabb appeared in the shadows of the scene. A local kid who sold newspapers downtown spotted them, and Rose called him over to them. He handed the lad ten dollars, a lot of money in those days, and told him to run across town to the Little Turf, the Maceos' first off-Seawall property at Twenty-Third and Avenue Q, and deliver a message to Sam. "Tell him we own downtown."[155]

The Maceos' business plan had never included snuffing out the competition, and the Crystal Club was no more considered competition than the tables at the Rio Grande farther west on Market or the craps and roulette games at the Rainbow Club on Twentieth Street or any of the other fifty-plus gambling dens on the island.[156] Neither were pinball or horseracing machines a threat to their ubiquitous nickel slots, and George Musey himself was no match in business or in reputation to the Maceos. The most logical reason for Musey's execution seems to have less to do with eliminating him and more to do with someone who was backing him—someone far more menacing whose interference would have endangered not only the Maceos but also the city itself. Someone who had just been sent an unambiguous message to stay out of Galveston.

7

THE CASE FOR CARLOS

Black Tuesday in November 1929 would linger in the minds of Americans as the day that marked their entrance into years of hardship and struggle. The Great Depression also spanned the decade in which Galveston's population swelled to nearly eighty thousand people and prosperity seemed as eternal as the tide rolling onto the beach. Bootlegging played a meaningful part in the island's early economic resilience, but the repeal of Prohibition put the responsibility squarely in the hands of the Maceos. Sam and Rose's glamorous Galveston was a soothing salve to the rest of the troubled state, and this kindness was generously rewarded by those seeking distraction and looking for luck. As the rest of the world was grounded with sobering reality, money was flying all over Galveston. The brothers would later provide the same buffer in the 1940s when the world went to war for the second time. Despite their ability to bring economic triumph to an entire city amid immeasurable adversity, certain shadows loom over the Maceos' history. These were cast from suppositions that vaguely and inaccurately calculate the extent of the family's immersion in the American Mafia.

Various sources refer to the Maceos as "mobbed up"[157] and "unsubtly tied up with the big underworld national combination,"[158] while others claim that the Maceo empire operated only with the permission of prestigious mafioso,[159] and still others claim that they were fiercely protective of Galveston and worked to keep the Mafia out of the city.[160] These preclusions contradict one another, except that they all trace back to one man—Carlos Marcello, the rising star and eventual don of the New Orleans Mafia. Interestingly, the sparse and scattered evidence that points to these three entirely different scenarios of Marcello's interaction with Galveston can be combined to create a fourth possibility. The real relationship between Marcello and the Maceos was most likely a patchwork of snippets from all the various theories, solidified by an awareness that Sam and Rose did in fact possess the circumstances and the finesse (and the finances) to work *with* the Mafia, even if they were neither members nor official associates of the Mafia—and to work with the Mafia and still want them to stay out of Galveston.

A handful of accounts are circulated throughout Galveston history that speak to the city's interactions with known mafioso, but they all end peacefully. Even Frank Nitti, who left town without paying Dutch and Johnny Jack their share of a $24,000 profit, was later found in Houston but was allowed to repay his debt with actual dollars (plus interest) instead of with his life.[161] When the Hollywood opened, Nitti was allegedly sent back to Texas by his boss, Al Capone, to case the situation. He was politely told to enjoy his evening at the club but to never return. Another Galveston legend speaks to a standoff at the causeway when Maceo's crew was alerted to some Chicago men who were on their way to the island. Nephew Anthony Fertitta raced across the drawbridge and had the operator raise it up to stop incoming traffic. He and a crew stationed themselves on the mainland side of the bridge to ensure that the men turned around before they even got to the bridge. After Johnny Jack Nounes was locked up, Capone became a customer of the Maceos during times when the Canadian whiskey well ran dry—the same situation that prompted Cleveland boss Moe Dalitz to forge a business partnership with Sam and Rose.[162] Albert Anastasia of New York was also said to have expressed interest in the Maceo enterprises without incident, but only once.[163]

The links to Carlos Marcello are equally tenuous and even less well known, yet they are also potent enough to be the real root of all speculation surrounding the Maceos' activities with the Mafia. Very little documentation exists, hence a tendency toward misinterpretation, but the puzzle pieces connect just enough to reveal only one plausible theory: Marcello needed Galveston and its waterways to negotiate his drug running, first with heroin and morphine from Cuba but then especially with marijuana from Mexico after it was criminalized in the United States in 1937. The Maceos let him use their territory, or at least chose not to interfere, and they may have even required him to compensate them financially, but they set clear boundaries. They were never to be connected to his outfit, and his drug selling and other interests in Galveston ended at the shoreline. If Sam and Rose did have this deal with Marcello, it appears to be one that they adopted rather than sought as a decorous compromise to a situation initially constructed by George Musey.

Sam and Rose were connected to New Orleans via their aunt, uncle and cousins who lived there long after Rose and company moved to Galveston. However, interstate travel was probably rare for a pair of barbers, and most of the family had migrated down the Gulf Coast by the mid-1920s. Later, the Maceos befriended the elite New Orleans hotelier Seymour Weiss, and they often stayed at his Roosevelt Hotel.[164] Musey's connections in New Orleans, on the other hand, were indisputably criminal, as he used them in the 1920s to hijack the Beach Gang's liquor trucks. Although Musey and Marcello's names never appear together in print, their timelines eerily intertwine. Carlos's early life was like Sam and Rose's; he was born in Sicily in 1910 and immigrated to New Orleans when he was an infant. But unlike the Maceos, Marcello took straightaway to the ongoing Sicilian crime wave in Louisiana. He had staged several clever, large-scale heists by the time he was in his late teens. His last at the age of twenty netted him $7,000 and nine years in the pen. Carlos was released in early 1935 after serving just longer than four years. Back on the bayou, Marcello opened a bar from which he peddled both booze and narcotics. His small-scale drug operation expediently expanded into a wholesale outfit that used shrimp boats as carriers from larger mother ships just as the rumrunners used their powerboats. Sicilians dominated the early shrimping industry in New Orleans since it was a common trade back home. This gave Carlos easy entrance into the business, a legitimate cover, huge piles of stinky seafood to conceal his cargo and access to the docks.[165] By the late 1930s, Marcello owned an entire fleet of shrimp boats that carried illegal narcotics up and down the Gulf Coast.[166]

Across the Gulf of Mexico, Musey had returned home in January 1934 and immediately went back to his hustle. Rumrunning was no longer an option, but the Maceos had shown themselves as willing to tolerate other vice operations so long as they did not cause any trouble or elicit any undue attention. Alluding to Musey's post-prison intentions is a documented purchase of high-quality gambling chips from the Mason Company of Chicago on November 16, 1934. The chips were inscribed with "Crystal," and the purchase was made by his brother Fred Musey, which aligns with his being named as the owner of the Crystal Club on Market Street when it was raided in 1935. A second purchase for Crystal casino chips was placed on March 15, 1935, which indicates that business was going well for the brothers, while an absence of any other orders

Sam Maceo (*center*) with Seymour Weiss (*right*). *Family collection.*

indicates that they did not appear to be opening any additional clubs.[167] Those affiliated with Musey claimed that he was killed only because he was imposing on the Maceos' business, but painting Sam and Rose as greedy and vengeful was more respectful to their friend's memory. However, Musey had been in business with his brother for eighteen months before he was executed.

Musey and Nounes were known during Prohibition to run their rum through the docks of Galveston. Since the port was the crux of Galveston's legitimate enterprises, this could not have been simply because the port was in the Downtown Gang's territory, so the gang must have been given de facto access by someone with influence. This arrangement appears to have been renewed after George Musey was freed, because soon after his death, rumors began to circulate that he was trying to "chisel out" a drug ring on the island.[168] Although investigators in 1931 and 1935 found no definitive links between George Musey and narcotics,[169] this does not dissolve his link to Marcello and hints to the possibility of a trade-off—access to the docks for backing on the streets.

Musey had been running a successful club with his brother for a year and a half. His trouble did not start until mid-1935, when he revealed a pronounced interest in pinball machines, which was the very topic of the business rendezvous Musey was conducting at the Alamo when he was gunned down. In the months immediately preceding Musey's slaying, a telling chain of events occurred. Carlos Marcello returned from prison, was officially inducted into the Mafia, began to run a large-scale narcotics operation and set up a business with his brother under the umbrella of Silver Dollar Sam Corolla, the present leader of the New Orleans syndicate. The business was called the Jefferson Music Company. It was a distributor of jukeboxes and pinball machines.[170]

A man who claimed to be a close associate of Musey's was interviewed by the press following his death, and he stated that "Musey was 'in the know' to such an extent that he was in a position to keep the whole town 'closed' if he felt he was not given fair treatment. He was prepared to put numerous coin operated machines, 'a thousand if he wanted to,' in operation as soon as the suffocating lid was removed from the island's languishing gaming activity."[171] Even with the partnership of Johnny Jack Nounes and an army of Downtown Gang soldiers, Musey was one of the first and hardest-hit casualties of the rum war. To claim himself as powerful enough to end the reign of Sam and Rose, the person with whom he was "in the know" must have been someone he viewed as far more powerful than the Maceos.

The idea that Musey's killing was carried out as more of a warning to Marcello than because of any threat Musey posed by himself, and that it was done as a warning rather than a potentially suicidal strategy to get rid of Marcello completely, is implied by the Maceos' continued yet furtive relationship with the New Orleans mobster even after Musey's death. First and foremost, nothing on the Gulf Coast from Brownsville to New Orleans happened without Sam and Rose knowing about it,[172] and drug rings were suspected in Galveston as late as the 1950s.[173] Furthermore, the Maceos possessed an intricate underground intelligence system that reached all the way to Austin. Often before anything would happen, the governor would find out and alert the Maceos, saying, "They're doing it again."[174]

In the mid-1930s, the City of Dallas took a cue from Galveston and went wide-open with prostitution and gambling to augment its failing economy. A common trend in Dallas was to run casino games out of hotel rooms, which is presumably what prompted the Maceos to purchase the Southland Hotel at 1200 Main Street. Only the name Maceo was inscribed on the deed, but investigators suspected that Carlos

Marcello was a partner, if not the majority or sole owner.[175] One of the first tenants at the Southland was future King of the Racketeers Benny Binion, whose violent and criminal inclinations emerged at the bright-eyed age of twenty-four. His earliest run-ins with the law were theft, weapons charges and two murder convictions.

In 1936, Dallas declared itself an open town just after the death of Benny's mentor Warren Diamond, former leader of the local gambling rackets, and Binion took his first step toward assuming Diamond's position by establishing headquarters and a craps game in room 226 of the Maceos' Southland Hotel. A sign on the door read "private," and at the push of a buzzer, a back alley–style window carved into the door slid open. A fog of cigarette smoke wafted around the doorman's face and oozed out the window as he visually screened the person requesting entrance. Inside, a suite of rooms included several dice tables, a bar and Benny's office where he grew the Southland Syndicate.[176] For Binion's business to succeed, however, he eventually had to make peace and share his profits with Carlos Marcello, who was expanding his empire into Dallas and other parts of Texas.[177] When one of Benny's henchmen, Johnny "Brazil" Grisaffi, was investigated by police, his phone records included a suspiciously large number of calls to Marcello's brother in New Orleans, but Grisaffi stated that he was merely ordering fish for his restaurant.[178]

Marcello's connection to the island, or at least the presence of drug running, is steeled by other suspicious incidents that occurred in Galveston in the 1930s. When Musey was captured in 1931, attempts were made to link him with the murder of Sam Lachinsky, an ex-con from Dallas whose body was found on West Beach and who was reported to be connected to the "dope racket."[179] In the August 1938 edition of *American Detective*, an article titled "Marijuana—Weed of Sin" blasted Galveston for its involvement with narcotics. Unapologetically sensational, the article referred to Galveston as the "Dope Gateway to Hell" and featured drawings in the style of graphic novels that depicted a woman with rage in her eyes and a marijuana cigarette in her mouth next to a man lying in a pool of blood with a knife in his back. Nevertheless, the article did contain sporadic morsels of seeming truth, such as the fact that the Federal Narcotics Unit had been fighting to take down a drug ring in Galveston since 1932. When an original copy of the publication was donated to the Rosenberg Library in Galveston, the benefactor attested to its rarity by claiming that upon its release, Sam Maceo had attempted to purchase every copy between the island and New Orleans. In addition to an outlandish tale of Rose being accused of murder (no charges were ever filed), they did correctly report that Sam was fighting narcotics charges in New York Federal Court.

When the police awakened Sam Maceo at his home on a crisp October morning in 1937, he thought he was being kidnapped. Fortunately, the arresting officers' credentials were valid, but Sam still managed to convince them that they did not need to take him in because he would drive himself to the station. Along the way, he picked up his friend and local newspaper columnist Christie Mitchell and gave him a ride downtown. Sam explained to the press, "I never mentioned it to him. I didn't think anything of it. I was innocent, so what should I be afraid of?" While the fifteen other locals who had been arrested on similar charges were held in jail cells until their bond hearings, Sam was permitted to wait in a nearby office. In total, eighty-seven people had been simultaneously indicted in a massive, nationwide dragnet that blanketed New York, Houston and New Orleans.[180] Sam's attorneys managed to delay his hearing and fight extradition for five years until he finally went to trial in New York City in October 1942. Some stories assert that his case was dismissed due to lack of evidence, but Sam Maceo was fully acquitted by a jury.

On the evening of October 23, 1942, after a brilliant defense led by Sam Maceo's ace attorney team of Louis C. Dibrell and George Wolf, a jury returned after hours of deliberation and said that they were unable to agree on a verdict for the Galveston magnate, though they were able to reach a verdict of guilty for Sam's codefendant and alleged coconspirator Joseph Schipano of New York. While Schipano was taken away to remit a $10,000 fine and serve a two-year sentence, the jury was escorted to a hotel where they were to sequester until resuming deliberations the next morning.[181] At ten o'clock the following morning, the jury of four women and eight men requested audience with the judge and told him that it would be impossible to reach a verdict unless they received clarification from the court regarding certain testimonies. The judge responded that they should remember their aim was to determine whether Maceo "was a member of this conspiracy" and dismissed them back to their deliberations. Wolf's immediate objection to these instructions was sustained, and the judge brought the jury back to the courtroom. The attorney refuted the judge's prior advice and explained to the jury in no uncertain terms that the "burden of proof was on the government." Out of eighty-seven indictments, only two defendants who claimed innocence had been acquitted. At the pronouncement of "not guilty," Sam openly wept. He then told reporters, "We are going back to Galveston as fast as we can."[182]

On the island, rumors surfaced that the narcotics found in Sam's car that led to his arrest were planted by a local prostitute, and local speculation surrounded not Sam's guilt but the identity of the person who set him up.[183] Even still, details imbedded in Sam's predicament subtly hint to the plausible scenario that the Maceos were doing their best to maneuver around a Marcello drug ring that had forced its way into Galveston waters via George Musey. The prosecutor in Sam's trial specifically claimed that Maceo went into narcotics trafficking in 1935.[184] In an earlier statement to the press, Sam alluded to his situation when he stated, "I have scrupulously kept the narcotic traffic out of our organization, as those acquainted with it will testify."[185]

Sam rarely drank and pronounced himself as having done as much as law enforcement to keep drugs out of Galveston. However, the likelihood of an arrangement with Marcello was not hypocrisy, rather it would reveal that the Maceos used their partnership to relegate his activities to the surrounding waterways, a theory augmented by the general perspective of residents during this time. Local drug use was viewed as such an anomaly that the "local dopehead" was the town jester. Furthermore, Sam's arrest on conspiracy charges was an aberrant shock to the community; civilians, local law enforcement and newspaper reporters heartily endorsed the notion that the Maceos were entirely independent and were not connected to anyone off the island.[186] Marcello was too powerful and well allied to be eliminated himself, but the Maceos were certainly shrewd enough to have known that the best way to keep him out of Galveston—the best way to control him—was to work with him.

After Sam was acquitted, Galveston disappeared almost completely from the eyeline of federal narcotics investigators, but in 1949, Carlos appeared to need another reminder. Marcello had been elected as the official don of the New Orleans Mafia in 1947 and was still in control of a large portion of Texas. In the early 1930s, a successful Houston rumrunner named Vincent Vallone decided to expand into gambling and nightclubs, but mediocre success led him to ally with the Maceos who hired him to manage their Houston club called the High Hat. Vallone was also arrested with Sam Maceo in the narcotics sweep of 1937, and although his charges were also dropped one year later, within two weeks he had been arrested for murder. He was convicted and sentenced to life in prison, but a full slate of distinguished men, including Rose Maceo and infamous New York mobsters Bugsy Siegel and Frank "The Prime Minister" Costello, testified as character witnesses in a 1946 appeal, the outcome of which was a full pardon for Vallone.[187]

Upon his release, Vallone managed a restaurant in Houston called the Villa Rosa, formerly operated by Dutch Voight, and he soon began work on a venue that appeared to require an investment far beyond his financial faculties. The Sorrento, named after the most beautiful town in his native Italian region of Calabria, was an extravagant three-hundred-seat restaurant and gambling club on the corner of Fannin and Bell in downtown Houston. The interior featured a 250-foot hand-painted wraparound mural that depicted intricate scenes of Italy. Unfortunately, Vallone would not live to see opening night.[188]

The lone eyewitness recounted a steamy July evening in 1949 when he was sitting on the front porch of his house located in the undeveloped areas of Houston along Chocolate Bayou Road. He noticed a black Cadillac speeding down the road toward his house and another dark sedan following closely behind. It almost looked as if the sedan was in pursuit of the Cadillac, but as the two vehicles came closer into view, the Cadillac began to slow down and pull over as if to let the other driver pass. As the sedan made its way around, the witness heard two quick blasts of a shotgun, after which the sedan sped away and the Cadillac slowly rolled to a stop on the side of the road. The witness walked tentatively over to the vehicle, its engine still running, and saw the man later identified as Vincent Vallone slumped over in the driver's seat.[189]

Harris County sheriff Buster Kern made a big to-do about the conspiracy behind the murder of Vincent Vallone, but most considered his theory laughable. Peter Duca, a peculiar man with a novelty shop at the Galveston airport, was said by Kern to be the don of the entire Texas Mafia and to have ordered the hit on Vallone. Two of Duca's out-of-town friends were beaten until they confessed to the sheriff's theory and the murder, but they later retracted their statements, claiming that they would have confessed to any crime if it made the beatings stop. Kern's accusation was enough, however, to establish a violation of the parole Duca had received upon release from prison for a previous murder, and he was arrested at a Dallas rail station after stepping off a train that had recently arrived from Galveston. Almost as if to prove that he was expendable and not the boss Kern thought he was, Duca was dead in his cell by the time a guard made his 8:45 p.m. rounds on the day of his arrest. Although the coroner recorded natural causes—heart failure—the timing clearly indicated murder.[190] Murder for retaliation perhaps, or possibly murder to prevent him from spilling the truth for a lighter sentence.

The Houston newspapers fielded an array of anonymous tips and printed the threats made by callers to Vallone's killer. One of these tips shined a spotlight directly on the island, and further investigations did reveal that in the days before his death, Vallone made a trip to Galveston. According to Vincent, Sam and Rose still owed him tens of thousands of dollars from a business venture prior to his incarceration, and he had come to collect. A statement of vengeance transcribed by the *Houston Press* sounded familiar to the claims after Musey's murder. "They thought Vallone was coming back into the rackets and because of his past power they were afraid of him."[191] Alternatively, Vincent Vallone's murder was more likely related to the fact that his last conversation was a phone call with Carlos Marcello.[192] At the very least, Marcello and the Maceos had an agreement—an agreement that the Maceos seemed determined to uphold despite Marcello's ruthless ambition. Their respective organizations would work together to keep the northern syndicates out of Texas, but they would also stay out of one another's way.[193]

In 1946, the leaders of the major American syndicates convened in Havana for a historic meeting with an attendance record that reads like a Mafia who's who. Meyer Lansky, Lucky Luciano, Frank Costello, Santo Trafficante, Moe Dalitz and Carlos Marcello all attended, and their known associate Frank Sinatra regaled the group with private performances.[194] Sam and Rose's names are noticeably absent from that list, and the only record of either one traveling to Cuba is a 1925 manifest upon which Rose's name appears, a trip that is more suitably timed with their rumrunning enterprises. This could be ascertained as their having a role within a hierarchy that put them under Marcello's control, but when Sam and Rose both passed away in the early 1950s, their authority was transferred to their cousin. Not even a Mafia don gets to appoint his successor, much less an associate.

The entire Maceo family worked in the business, but that was the only aspect that was "organized" in their crime. They did not exploit or extort people, nor did they attempt to control the waste management companies or monopolize the municipal and commercial construction industries by owning all the steel and concrete factories like the major urban syndicates.[195] In 1976, the *San Antonio Express* ran a somewhat anachronistic article titled "The Mob Is Moving into Texas." Marcello was mentioned but was only given claim to Dallas. The lone reference to Galveston was an entirely separate, reminiscent paragraph about Sam and Rose, more than twenty years after their deaths. No matter the protestations or conjecture, in the end, this empire was all Maceo.

8

GAMBLER'S PARADISE

Established in 1932, the Turf Athletic Club was a parent company, but more accurately, it was the mother of all the various gambling enterprises offered by the Maceos.[196] The name itself implied their desire to create a big-city gambling scene in Galveston. Echoing a parallel to the dirt and sod combination used at racetracks, *turf* was commonly used to designate large gambling dens in New York City. The Maceos' non-gambling operations, such as the restaurant and entertainment portions of the Sui Jen and the Hollywood and a myriad of other venues and businesses, operated on paper as autonomous entities, not subsidiaries of the Turf. The gambling chips circulating throughout their different clubs illustrate this structure. "TAC" was emblazoned on all of the casino chips, and the initials of the specific location where it could be used were inscribed underneath. Chips that read "TURF" were universal and could be used at any location. Hearkening to the success of the TAC and thus the legitimacy of the Maceo gambling empire as perceived by locals, their casino chips, no matter the inscription, were as good as cash and accepted as legitimate currency by Galveston retailers.[197]

The TAC's first headquarters were located inside Ollie Quinn's DeLuxe Club, but the company soon acquired a building in the 2200 block of downtown that spanned from 2210 to 2216 Market Street. The interior of the three-story structure evolved like all Maceo endeavors, from its early form that only occupied the first of three floors to a multilevel entertainment complex. At first, the front room housed only a slot machine depot, behind

Above, left: Turf casino chip. *Author's private collection.*

Above, right: Turf Athletic Club casino chip with "SL" for Studio Lounge. *Anonymous private collection.*

Left: Turf Athletic Club casino chip with "WR" for Western Room. *Anonymous private collection.*

which was a pool hall. Behind the pool hall was a large, hidden anteroom off the alleyway that hosted a twenty-four-hour sports book. After the building was raided by axe-wielding Texas Rangers in 1935, it underwent extensive renovations that built out all three floors for legitimate businesses to front the back-room operations.[198]

Placed on the first floor with an entrance numbered 2214 was a fine-dining restaurant called the Turf Grill that became well-known for its gourmet menu with a sophisticated style and level of service that encapsulated "the joy of better living." An electric eye was installed above the front entry so that the door would automatically open for guests, but people kept walking on the wrong side and getting hit by the door, so the entire contraption was removed and replaced with the first revolving door in Texas.[199] To its right was a cigar stand and then another storefront that eventually became the Turf Tap Room, which served an extensive selection of beer and casual,

Left: Rare photograph of 2210–2216 Market, TAC headquarters and home of the Turf Grill, Studio Lounge, Turf Tap Room and the Western Room. At the back was a sports betting parlor. *Rosenberg Library*.

Opposite: A 1948 advertisement for the Turf Grill. Galveston Isle *magazine, Rosenberg Library*.

pub-style food. To the left of the revolving door at 2216 was an ingress leading to a ridiculously slow elevator, which was the only way to get to the second floor.

The limited and prolonged access to the second floor was a manufactured stalling device in the event of a visit from law enforcement. Located on the second floor was the Studio Lounge, which originally consisted of elegant clubrooms that hosted wedding receptions and fashion shows and moonlighted as a late-night poker den. In later years, the Studio Lounge was redesigned and became a premier nightlife venue. Adjacent to the Studio Lounge, a Wild West–themed gambling room called the Western Room was opened in 1950. On the third floor, oddly enough, was an actual gymnasium with a boxing ring, athletic equipment and mats for tumbling, as well as a pool hall and other rooms used for business meetings and conferences.[200]

The TAC building also housed the company's administrative offices. On the third floor was a large accounting room and offices that eventually served as the base of the Maceos' real estate conglomerate, Gulf Properties Incorporated. Additional office space was located on the first floor, including a cashier booth with check-cashing services that were referred to as the "weekend bank of Galveston."[201] The booth adjoined two small offices; one was the workspace of Sam Serio and Joe T. Maceo, and the

other, called the safe room, contained two large safes that concealed a third, smaller private safe.[202] These offices were the hub of the financial ebb and flow of both the casino and the coin-operated dealings. A group of young boys would hang around the front of the TAC building during the day, waiting to be chosen as a runner or errand boy. Often, they would

Above: Linen napkins from the Studio Lounge and Balinese Room. *Anonymous private collection.*

Left: Matchbooks from the Studio Lounge and Balinese Room. *Anonymous private collection.*

be trusted to transport operating cash between the office and the Sui Jen. This arrangement was beneficial for the boys' families in its provision of extra income, and it was beneficial to the Maceos because hardly anyone would suspect that a sack lunch carried by a schoolboy running down Twenty-Second Street was, in fact, a paper bag stuffed with thousands of dollars in cash.

In perfect contrast to the glitzy gambling halls that catered to elite out-of-towners was the betting parlor off the alleyway that catered to the everyman, all day every day. The air was thick with cigarette smoke that gave way only to the stench of hard liquor. Chairs were scattered among a sea of white created from waves of tip pulls and betting forms that originated from the ticket counter staffed by twelve to fifteen men dressed

A 1949 advertisement for the Turf Tap Room. Galveston Isle *magazine, Rosenberg Library.*

in starched white button-down shirts with black ties and black trousers. Stretched along the entire expanse of the wall behind the pit were huge billboards that listed baseball scores, race results and betting odds. In addition to attending to the on-site bettors who would often linger in the betting parlor for hours listening to sporting events or horse races when they were broadcast live, the booking agents would also field telephone bets taken any time of the day, provide security if it was needed and perform credit checks for the cashiers at the other Maceo outposts. The Maceos' recordkeeping was so comprehensive that casinos all over the country used it to screen their customers.[203]

Aided by the height of technology at the time, a wire ticker-tape system that connected two hundred cities in thirty-five states, the back room of the Turf building became the biggest horse-betting parlor in the state of Texas during the Great Depression. The racing wire was the invention of Moses L. Annenberg, whose Nationwide News Service was supplemented by hardware from the American Telegraph and Telephone Company. It provided instant results and outcomes of sporting events and races from all over the nation. The TAC fielded bets for football, basketball and baseball games, as well as

Flatware from the Turf Grill. *Anonymous private collection.*

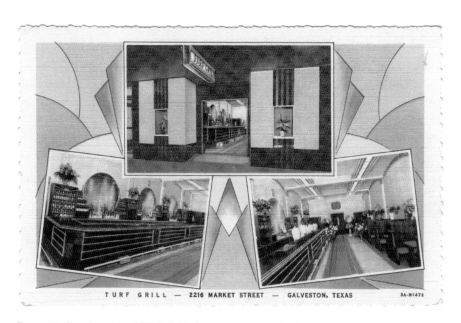

Postcard of the interior of Turf Grill. *Anonymous private collection.*

for both horse- and dog-racing tracks, but these activities were not confined to Market Street. Maceo establishments throughout Galveston County served as satellite betting stations, and several third-party businesses kept Maceo books for a 25 percent cut of the profit.[204]

Another popular amusement at the Turf was a simple lottery known as tip-books or tip-pulls. A small book with 120 pieces of sequentially numbered pages was passed around the room. At ten cents apiece, gamblers could purchase and then pull as many tips from the book as they desired. When all of the pages had been bought and pulled, a winning number was drawn and awarded with 80 percent of the pot—a two-to-ten-dollar split with the house. The frivolity, decent odds and low buy-in of the live lottery tip-pulls were a huge draw, and they became so ubiquitous in Galveston that the island was gifted with yet another title, Tip Book Capital of the U.S.[205]

In 1937, Rose uncharacteristically took a brief turn at center stage when he publicly announced the purchase of Crystal Palace for $140,000, the largest financial transaction on Galveston's beachfront in years. The first floor of the massive bath- and playhouse on the Seawall featured a 50-by-140-foot saltwater swimming pool, and the upper two floors contained eight hundred dressing rooms, a photo booth, a shooting gallery, a bowling alley, a café, an open-air amphitheater and a 9,000-square-foot dance floor. The structure was crowned with a beautiful rooftop garden that offered panoramic views of the Gulf.

Constructed in 1916, the Crystal needed updating by the time it was sold to the Maceos. Improvements were promised to the public by way of large-scale modernization and the addition of Turkish and hot baths, but discreetly installed on the upper floors was a nightclub/casino called the

Casino chip from the Galveston Texas Beach Club. *Author's personal collection.*

Galveston Texas Beach Club, with Vic A. "Gigolo" Maceo as its manager.[206] Vic lost his father, Sam and Rose's brother Frank, when he was only ten years old, but he was close to his uncles and started his career under their watch as an eighteen-year-old roulette dealer at the Hollywood Dinner Club. Under Vic's direction, the Beach Club became a wildly popular late-night spot for beachgoers, but by 1949, the decrepit Palace had suffered all the salt air it could bear and was finally demolished. With a captivating countenance, infectious sense of humor and sharp intellect,

Vic A. "Gigolo" Maceo posing in front of the Hollywood Dinner Club where he started in the family business as a roulette dealer. *Family collection.*

Vic A. was not stymied by the end of the gambling era and went on to become independently successful as a real estate investor.[207]

The growth of the Maceo realm was temporarily obstructed in 1939 when the Hollywood was raided for the last time and permanently padlocked. The severity of this blow, however, was nullified by the inspiration it elicited. The firsthand education Sam received on the American judicial system became a distinct advantage in designing a raid-proof club. Sam learned that law

Above: Side view of the original Balinese Room, circa 1942. Guests had to walk down a six-hundred-foot covered pier to get to the club. *Rosenberg Library*.

Left: TAC was emblazoned above the original entrance to the Balinese Room foyer, where a host would screen potential guests and make sure they were members. *Rosenberg Library*.

enforcement officers could not search beyond their line of sight without a warrant and that they could not get a warrant without evidence. And without evidence, he could not be charged. All he needed was a gambling room that could be converted into a game room and, most importantly, enough time to complete the conversion. Construction began on the Sui Jen property, and a six-hundred-foot covered pier was erected that dead-ended into a T-shaped structure hovering over the Gulf on pilings. The base of the *T* would house a dining room and ballroom, and the gambling rooms would be at the head, accessible through a long hallway and a series of glass doors. Hidden discreetly in the corners of the gaming room were alarm bells hardwired to a button in a foyer located just off the sidewalk. The letters *TAC* were etched above the door where a maître d' catechized potential guests. Only members of the club and law enforcement were permitted to pass through to the covered walkway, the latter of which was secretly announced by a push of the button and a sound of the alarm.

At first, the revamp was to be an expansion of the Sui Jen that further embellished its Asian motif, but one month before the grand opening came "a date which will live in infamy." On Sunday, December 7, 1941, at 7:48 a.m. Hawaiian time, Imperial Japan launched an aerial attack on Pearl Harbor. More than 350 aircraft decimated the naval base in Honolulu, killing 2,335 military personnel and 68 civilians and wounding a total of 1,178 others. An American population that was previously unsupportive of involvement in the ongoing war was quick to unleash a resounding battle cry steeped in nationalism, and the United States formally entered World War II the next day. Sensitive to the country's suffering, Sam Maceo knew that public opinion had suddenly altered his thematic premise, taking it from novel and exotic to nearly treasonous. Without hesitation, Sam yet again conquered chaos with creativity and ordered a complete redesign of the new club.

Fortunately, his designer Virgil Quadrie[208] was both a genius and a magician, and within one month he completely transformed the club with a new South Pacific tropical theme that played on the paradisiacal elements of Galveston's cityscape but elevated them with the romance and mystery of remote lands. He mounted four glittering, ten-foot-tall copper and neon palm trees on each corner of the dance floor and wrapped the dining room with surrealistic murals of oversized flowers and shapely women in grass skirts dancing among the white sand and azure water of Bali beaches—hand-painted by Quadrie himself. White leather booths sat atop intertwining palm fronds patterned on the carpet, ivory telephones gleamed under the soft yellow glow of elaborate wall sconces and crystal chandeliers[209] and the neutral walls were textured with a façade of metal cladding panels in a geometric pattern. Black lights above the dance floor shone down through draped fishnets and glass globes, making the sequined gowns and starched white tuxedo shirts strobe as patrons glided past the tables.[210] A giant aquarium spanned the entire wall of an adjacent lounge that was decorated in a striking palette of oranges and reds. Immaculately groomed servers attended the guests' every whim while tuxedo-clad dealers greeted gamblers as they entered a resplendent back room trimmed in red velvet and bathed in bright white light. The club was also a technical marvel. Using the latest innovations, sound engineer Al Olson wired a series of speakers that were completely hidden from view,[211] and Quadrie mounted tiny twinkling lights in the painted blue ceiling to resemble stars.[212] On opening day, January 17, 1942, wonder and amazement struck the hearts of all who beheld the Balinese.

Early Balinese Room casino chips.
Anonymous private collection.

Quadrie also coined a new name for the club as he clothed the interior in tropical luxury, but the design of the Balinese Room was as clever as it was beautiful. Behind the bar were trap doors where liquor bottles could be dumped into the waters below, and concealed compartments were positioned throughout the club in hidden rooms and fake walls. In the gambling hall, certain tables were hinged to the wall and could be folded up like Murphy beds, while the surfaces of other tables would be overlaid with cloth to look like bridge, backgammon and pool tables. A large dummy oven was put in the kitchen, and its only purpose was to hide suitcases of casino chips. If the alarm sounded, everyone remained calm but swiftly launched into covert mode. The pit boss quietly requested that the gamblers pocket or purse their chips and the waiters whizzed around the room with trays of pre-prepped soda and exchanged them for the glasses of liquor on the tables.

Sam Maceo (*back left*) posing with his wife Edna and a group of guests at a table inside the Balinese. One of the large palm trees on a corner of the dance floor is behind Sam's right shoulder. *Rosenberg Library.*

Each busboy, cook and dealer was assigned a specific plan of action, and the choreographed transformation took barely three minutes.

In the case of a landlocked club, one minute would not have been a fast-enough conversion, but the Balinese walked on water. Texas Rangers had to cover six hundred feet of pier to get to it, and the expansive covered walkway was sardonically dubbed "Ranger Run" in their honor. The Rangers also had to cross the spacious dining and dancing room before they reached the back, thus performers did their part to add a few crucial seconds to the clock by striking up "The Eyes of Texas" in "tribute" to the visiting lawmen. Since the eyes of Texas were literally upon them, guests did what any good and decent (and sarcastic) Texan would do and responded by rising from their seats to pay their respects, which not coincidentally made it much more difficult for the Rangers to navigate their way to the gaming hall. By the time the Rangers made it to the back room, patrons were engaged in games of bridge, dominoes and billiards and sipping on soda pop like a cat washing down the canary.

On March 6, 1943, seven lawmen were able to scrape together enough peripheral evidence to obtain a warrant to raid the Balinese, but a three-hour search netted nothing more than a lackluster collection of liquor bottles that barely totaled a half-case.[213] By-the-drink charges for operating an open saloon were threatened after the raid but were never filed, and the embarrassingly miniscule findings were enough to make future judges shy

Top: Wooden matches imprinted with Studio Lounge and Balinese Room. *Anonymous private collection.*

Bottom: Back cover of the matchbooks. *Anonymous private collection.*

away from signing a warrant. Those who did sign them were often known to do so enthusiastically and then immediately pick up the phone to alert the Maceo outfit or the Galveston mayor that the law was on its way. For the majority of the next two decades, the raid-proof Balinese Room would operate uninterrupted, and its operators would remain unscathed.

Sam and his staff ran a first-class operation on all fronts. Coarse language, excessive drunkenness and raucous behavior were not tolerated. Standard business hours were 8:00 p.m. to 2:00 a.m., but the schedule would extend far into the morning for the right gambler and a big enough bet. Only self-employed Galvestonians were allowed in the club, not as a classist gesture but as a protective one. The Maceos were primarily focused on drawing the big-money players from Houston and beyond to parlay Galveston to a level of state- and nationwide acclaim that was far more beneficial and significantly less risky to the community than chasing a single jackpot.[214] If a local resident did somehow manage to overextend himself, arrangements were made to discreetly pull him off the table. Quite often, the debt would be quietly forgiven, followed by, "I don't want to see you here again."[215] In one specific occurrence, a father showed up to the cashier's station to pay his son's debt. Sam Maceo shooed him away and said, "Just make sure he never comes back."[216] Maceo clubs were not a twenty-four-hour

Postcard featuring the interior of the Balinese Room, circa 1950s. *Anonymous private collection.*

leeching like modern-day Vegas, where the percentages are calculated. The goal was for guests to be entertained, to enjoy themselves and, most of all, to have fun. Except for rare instances, the games produced no big winners and no big losers. The graciousness and heightened etiquette of Sam Maceo and company generated the devotion of Galvestonians while also creating a cultured yet whimsical ambiance that was savored by the entire region's upper stratum.

Although the oil boom of the early twentieth century gave Houston a distinct advantage over Galveston and initiated a growth rate that would forever outpace the island city, it also provided a deep well of clientele for the Maceos, who made the island's commercial loss its economic gain. Black gold millionaires were frequent guests of the Balinese Room, including two rags-to-riches oilmen, Glenn McCarthy and Hugh Roy Cullen. R.H. Abercrombie once lost $30,000 in one visit. Jack Josey, known by employees of the Balinese as "Mr. J,"[217] was an independent oil speculator who defied the odds when he invested in the unforeseeable value of what is now the posh city of Lakeway, Texas. He was known to drop $80,000 to $150,000 in a night. Members of Houston's Jewish community who loved to gamble would descend upon the island in droves when Jewish entertainers such as Sophie Tucker or the Ritz Brothers were in town. High rollers came from as far away as Oklahoma City, St. Louis, Mexico and Puerto Rico to gamble in the back rooms.[218] No matter their origin, the resounding sentiment among guests of Sam Maceo was that they always lost money but loved every minute of it.[219]

Gambling was not a requirement for membership to the Balinese Room. In the dining room, the cuisine, atmosphere and especially the entertainment were enough to lure high-profile state and national politicians. Sam T., also known as Little Sammie, once told a reporter, "We had the pros working for us. The best dealers, the best bartenders, the best waitresses. The finest chefs."[220] This side of the Balinese was also accessible to the general public. A meal could run for as little as four dollars, but it provided admission to some of the hottest acts in the nation.[221] According to one *Galveston Daily News* reporter in 1965, the Maceos "had gambling to support the high cost of entertainment. Or high-priced entertainment to support the profits of gambling. Opinions vary."[222]

The majority of the Maceos' entertainment roster was filled with local and area bands, pianists and singers who would play the hits of the era and were tasked with keeping the dance floor full. The big-name acts only performed about three times per year.[223] Historically, however, the Hollywood, Balinese and Studio Lounge are remembered for hosting nationally famous acts with exorbitant pay scales; the Maceos were known to spend as much as $18,000 to $20,000 in one week for entertainment. The Ritz Brothers drew $13,000 per week, and Sophie Tucker, $10,000. Other famous acts of the time included Ted Weems, Jimmy Dorsey, Bob Crosby, Ben Pollack, Ship Fields and Ray Noble.[224] Victor Lombardo, who played in his brother Guy Lombardo's orchestra at the Hollywood Dinner Club's debut, returned with his own thirteen-piece band to play the Balinese in 1948.[225]

In the late 1940s, Virgil Quadrie led a redesign of the Studio Lounge in the TAC building, which rivaled his work at the Balinese. Lavishly redecorated in ultramodern art deco, Quadrie used zebra skins, large mirrors and bizarrely beautiful light fixtures to complement the wildly printed, fireproof carpet. When a blacklight was switched on, it would reveal an entirely different pattern.[226] The layout of the Studio Lounge was intended to be much more personal and intimate than the Balinese, but it also lent a feeling of solidarity, much like a high-

Postcard depicting Murdoch's (*foreground*) and the new six-hundred-foot Balinese Pier. *Author's personal collection.*

Singer Gertrude Niesen with Rose Maceo (*far right*) dining at the Balinese Room during her stay in Galveston when she performed at the Studio Lounge. *Rosenberg Library.*

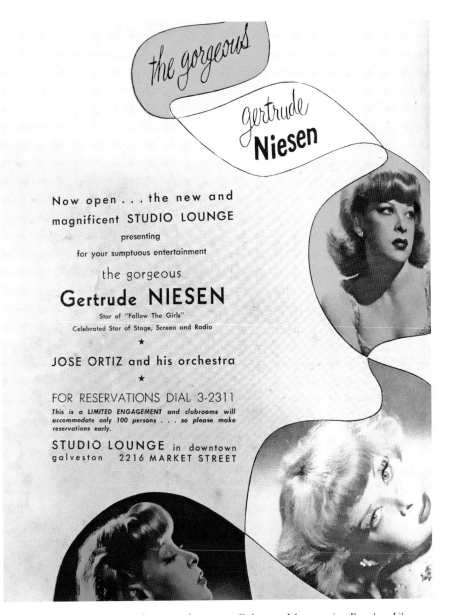

Advertisement for Gertrude Niesen performance. Galveston Isle *magazine, Rosenberg Library.*

scale, back-alley cabaret with tables close together, "love nest" booths dotting the perimeter and lush, interchangeable draperies that could be manipulated depending on the mood of the evening. Surrealistic murals on the walls were "a touch of Matisse and a bit of Cezanne and a little of Picasso." Quadrie remarked to journalist Christie Mitchell that he was "prouder of this than anything I have ever done." His jaw-dropping creation was the backdrop for performances by A-list starlets Peggy Lee and Gertrude Niesen.[227]

Renowned bandleader Phil Harris began performing in Galveston in 1933 and became a close friend of the Maceo family, appearing regularly at their clubs well into the 1950s. He received his first national exposure on one of Sam's famous live radio broadcasts, which catapulted him to stardom, and Harris repaid the kindness by producing massive media exposure for Galveston. He was called "Galveston's no. 1 ambassador of goodwill" and regularly used his celebrity to publicize the island in interviews, on radio shows and at live performances. In September 1941, press outlets from all over the country came to Galveston when he married Hollywood actress and singer Alice Faye in a seventh-floor suite at the Hotel Galvez.[228] Harris also once drew nearly twenty thousand fawning fans to the Seawall for a free concert hosted by the Maceos.[229]

The most enduringly famous artist to grace Galveston was Frank Sinatra, although his visits were more personal than professional. He befriended the Maceo family sometime in the 1940s, and although the accounts of Sinatra appearing on the island logically give way to the assumption that he performed, he never sang a note in Galveston. Known for cultivating friendships with an array of famous American

Frank Sinatra sitting with Sam Maceo (*far right*) and Anthony Fertitta (*far left*) when he was visiting the island in 1949. *Family collection.*

Mafia figures and bosses based on a mutual love of money and gambling, Sinatra's vast and volatile network was not always an advantage. When he was in Galveston, he was usually hiding out from a disgruntled "friend." During Sinatra's stay, he would sometimes dine with Sam at the Balinese for publicity, but the rest of the time he stayed hidden at Grandma Maceo's house, out of the public eye.[230]

Gambling, booze and entertainment were the crux of the family business, but the urbane and ultra-sophisticated manner in which these were presented was a distinct Maceo trademark. Without it, they would have been merely another set of tawdry underground vice-peddlers. That did not necessarily make the business right, but it sure was proper.[231] The real power behind their business strategy was that it also formed the philosophy by which they lived. Sam's ability to make anyone feel like a king was not exclusively displayed to big-shot gamblers but was also available to the destitute and downtrodden. Rose's keen financial maneuvering was not merely a benefit to the partners of TAC, but it was also a boon to all of the businessmen in Galveston. The Maceo vision enveloped and ingratiated an entire island.

9

BEYOND THE BALINESE

Before the Maceos, Galveston's main source of prominence was a burgeoning international port of commerce that was substantiated by the cotton trade and the subsequent banking and insurance industries. Although the city's economy produced several millionaires in the late 1800s, it was predominantly controlled by three families: the Moodys, Kempners and Sealys. These families did a lot of good for Galveston in aggressively perpetuating its stance as one of the top-producing ports in the world. Additionally, after the 1900 storm, patriarch I.H. "Ike" Kempner singlehandedly restructured the defunct city government to a commission form of government that was adopted by other American cities. Unfortunately, the commission was also prone to corruption and eventually served as a satellite battleground where the Moodys warred with the allied Kempners and Sealys for influence. Within a decade, a city built on the prowess of self-made men was no more. The dominance of the Big Three had turned into a chokehold bound by nepotism and political manipulation, driving out anyone who dared dip a toe in the trifold's pool. Many of the exiles went to Houston and made it the largest city in the South, while Galveston continued to cannibalize itself into near obscurity.[232] But the Maceos changed all of that.

Sam and Rose not only forged a path where there was none prior but also wrestled influence with such delicate precision that the Big Three developed a form of Stockholm syndrome and became smitten with their usurpers. Any member of the three families needed only to make one phone

Wax cups illustrated with different Maceo businesses, used for holding chips in the casino. *Author's personal collection.*

call to shut the Maceos down, but in the better part of forty years, that call was never made.[233] All three dynasties certainly skimmed the cream off the top as the Maceos churned, but to their credit, they also cared about their hometown. The familial hierarchy was wise enough to know that the Maceos were good for Galveston, and even if they would never admit it, they knew that Sam and Rose had achieved something even they were not able to do. The Maceos were never fully accepted into their realm of high society—Sam was denied membership to the Galveston Country Club—but an unspoken undercurrent of respect and appreciation was demonstrated with extensive behind-the-scenes business dealings and frequent patronage of their restaurants and clubs.[234]

Unlike commerce on the harbor side, the Maceos proved that the entertainment business was inelastic given the right leadership. It was not subject to the whims of the U.S. economy nor did it have to be limited to the summer season, as much of the population previously assumed. During the Great Depression, unemployment in Galveston was practically nonexistent, and the hotels were at capacity, even in the winter. During World War II, rations and scarcity were the norm across the nation but not on the island. The starlit clubs were more than businesses, they were also marketing tools. In fact, the restaurants themselves rarely broke even on the balance sheet. Of course, they were more than solvent after adding in the gambling revenue, but their real purpose was to make the island as famous as the voices that lilted out of the Balinese.[235] The clubs were the siren songs, but instead of crashing against the rocks, those who followed the elusive music found a kaleidoscopic carnival on the seaside that was graciously augmented with tropical "fruit machines," tip-books and bookies. If attendance lagged for any reason, Sam would call one of his crooners to perform an outdoor concert on the Seawall, free and open to the public.

Maceo holdings thus expanded far beyond the Balinese Room and Turf Athletic Club. In addition to performers, Sam underwrote the first legal and professional boxing matches in Texas, held on the third floor of the TAC building. Gigolo Maceo worked as a boxing promoter for Houston-area fighting talent.[236] The Maceos sponsored an annual Oleander Bowl football game, and they are credited with giving Jimmy Demaret his start on the professional golf circuit. They hosted pool tournaments and invited national billiards champions for showcases and demonstrations.[237]

On the Seawall, Splash Day had been put on pause during the Depression but was fully reinvigorated in the 1940s. In 1948, it drew seventy-five thousand people over the course of one weekend, and a Saturday crowd of twenty-five thousand lined the Seawall for a mile to watch a Splash Day exhibition featuring a Bell Helicopter and a local daredevil, Bob DeWild. The dramatic four-hour display began with flight maneuvers but peaked when DeWild grabbed hold of a trapeze dangling from the chopper. It carried him over the water and stopped just east of the Balinese, hovering one hundred feet above the Gulf of Mexico. DeWild performed several stunts on the trapeze to raucous cheers, but the crowd went silent when he readied himself to jump into the crashing waves below. After a few final tricks, DeWild released his grip and "dropped like a marble statue." A hushed concern rippled through the crowd in the seconds it took him to resurface, and the deafening applause at the sight of his bobbing head grew even louder when the helicopter swung low over DeWild, paused long enough for him to grab hold of the trapeze and hoisted him out of the water.[238]

The Maceos' Derby Amusement Company leased the land at Twenty-Fifth and Seawall Boulevard for the Great American Racing Derby, a carousel-style horse "race." Life-size horses placed parallel to each other moved up and down on slotted platforms that revolved around a circular track. The horses were pulled back and forth in their slots by a system of cables under the platform, which resulted in one horse reaching the finish line slightly ahead of the others. This horse was declared the winner.

Phil Harris tells local boxer Eddie Bertalino, "I betcha I can take it." Galveston Isle *magazine, Rosenberg Library.*

The Maceo family at a Mardi Gras ball. (*Left to right*) Mr. and Mrs. Rose Maceo, Mr. and Mrs. Anthony Fertitta, Vic A. "Gigolo" and Mrs. Frank Maceo. *Family collection.*

Murdoch Bathhouse Company was another Maceo subsidiary that owned the longstanding island institution on the beachside at Twenty-Third and Seawall. In addition to the bathhouse, it included Murdoch Bingo and Murdoch Sportsland, a shooting gallery. After the Derby was dismantled, the Beach Amusement Park operated another fun-land on the Boulevard at Twenty-Fourth and Twenty-Fifth Streets. The Miss Hollywood was a charter party boat company, and a mammoth bingo hall called Playland was located at 6102 Broadway.[239]

Entertainment aside, the diverse Maceo portfolio included immense real estate investments that were eventually incorporated as Gulf Properties and another investment firm called the San Luis Corporation. Early on, Sam and Rose's real estate deals were often instigated by their coin-operated machines under the banners Gulf Vending Company and Galveston Novelty Company. If they wanted their fruit machines in a specific location, they would simply buy the building and include the slots as a verbal stipulation of the commercial lease. Later, the larger portion of their land holdings were not leased.

The Maceos had the Little Turf at Twenty-Third and Avenue Q, the Bird Cage, the Moulin Rouge, the Fish House and the Chili Bowl managed by Vincent A. Maceo. The Corner at Twenty-First and Mechanic Streets opened in 1950 and featured a tap room and oyster bar. The Sportsman's Club, located off the bayou at Sixty-Eighth and Broadway, was a low-key establishment on the outskirts of town that is reported to have offered respite and anonymity to various visiting underground characters. Little Sammie managed the Streamline Dinner Club and the Silver Moon Dinner Club in Dickinson, a favorite haunt of oil tycoons that was known for mouthwatering steaks and was one of several off-island Maceo properties throughout the county. Kemah had the Edgewater Lounge and the Kemah Den, while LaMarque and Texas City kept an impressive collection of their slots and sports books. Residents of Houston joked that a southbound trip to the island included crossing the "Maceo-Dickinson Line" into Galveston County.[240]

Throngs of people on Seawall Boulevard, circa 1940. *Rosenberg Library*.

Left: Gambling chip from the Edgewater Lounge in Kemah, Texas. *Author's personal collection.*

Below: Sam's World War II draft card lists his address as the Galvez Hotel and names Gulf Properties at 2214 Market Street. *Ancestry.com.*

Brick-and-mortar investments were supplemented by an array of others—service entities like the Stewart Beach Catering Company and the Maceo Catering Company, as well as the Modern Music Company, sometimes called the M&M Music Company, which distributed jukeboxes. The Maceos owned a construction outlet called M&M Building Corporation, as well as the Vernell Liquor Partnership and two equipment companies, the Dickinson Equipment Company and Turf Stores with warehouses at 2027 Strand Street.

In 1934, Sam Maceo purchased a parcel for consideration in the Crescent Oil Syndicate No. 1 Shaw on Galveston Island and found his way into big oil. He formed Gulf Oil Properties and, eventually, Sam Maceo Oil Operations and the General Crude Oil Company. Sam entrenched himself in this arena and was known to pace the floor all night, waiting for word on the results of the latest drill. This feverish obsession is said to have led to Sam's diminishing interest in the entertainment portion of his career and may have prompted his willingness to cede the position of club manager to two of his nephews in the mid-1940s. But as much as he loved the risk and adventure of oil, Sam was most passionate about his labor of love, a magazine called the *Galveston Isle*, which launched in 1948. His close friend Christie Mitchell wrote often for the publication, which was used to promote and pride Galveston as a premiere entertainment destination.

Most of the Maceo money stayed on the island. Apart from travel and the occasional—or in Sam's case, regular—custom-tailored suit from New York City, the Maceos shopped local and lived local. Their deposits were made to local banks, all of the Maceos owned property in Galveston and four of them aided in the expansion of the residential areas by building family homes in the newly formed Denver Court neighborhood behind Fort Crockett on the Seawall. Sam, again, was the lone exception. He resided in an upper suite of the Hotel Galvez, owned in part by the Kempner families, but in line with his closer affiliation, he later moved his family to the Moody-owned Buccaneer Hotel (now demolished) one block away. All of the Maceo children attended Galveston schools, and local suppliers outfitted Maceo homes and businesses. Maceo employees, which numbered twenty-five hundred at their peak, lived, shopped and dined in Galveston.[241] The hundreds of thousands of visitors brought to the island

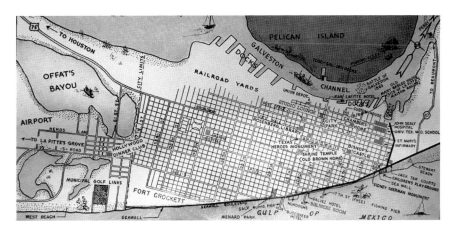

Tourist map printed in the back of *Galveston Isle*. *Rosenberg Library.*

Monkey Business 10

Galveston's Gift to Government 12

PUBLISHER   SAM MACEO
EDITOR   EDWIN E. LLEWELLYN
MANAGING EDITOR   ANTHONY FERTITTA

CONTRIBUTING EDITORS
    NATALIE MOSKOWITZ, C. MITCHELL,
    O. DODSON, TERRY MacLEOD
ART DIRECTOR   HARRY CONGDON

GALVESTON ISLE is published by the Galveston
Isle Publishing Company, Inc., with offices at
2216 Market St., Galveston, Texas. Sam Maceo,
President; Edwin E. Llewellyn, Vice-President;
Sam Serio, Secretary-Treasurer.

Above: Docket for *Galveston Isle* magazine. *Rosenberg Library*.

Opposite: The 1940 federal census showing Sam Maceo as a resident of the Hotel Galvez.
Later, he would move to the Buccaneer after his marriage to Edna Sedgwick. *Ancestry.com*.

each year, either directly or indirectly by Maceo marketing, created an insatiable demand for restaurants, lodging and recreation that launched hundreds of new businesses and jobs, increased the profits and pay scales of those existing and, in turn, inflated Galveston's resident population.

The Maceos also philanthropically funneled their wealth back to the island. In 1950 alone, Sam and Rose donated $50,000 ($500,000 today) to seventy-five different charities and organizations, and that was only what was on record. Regular beneficiaries were St. Mary's Catholic Cathedral and the First Baptist Church. Rose gave a large portion of his fortune to underprivileged children, and Sam was known for giving people opportunities more often than cash. He offered budding entrepreneurs a leg-up and discreetly paid for the college tuition of several local teens.[242] Quiet contributions such as these were as common as the Maceos' support of organizations. Sam once heard of an African American family who had a system of buckets that they would set around the house whenever it rained. They had been doing this so long that everyone knew exactly where the buckets had to go. Unprompted, Sam sent a construction crew over to install a new roof on their house. He did the same for a nearby church, and once, when a local car dealer was on the brink, Sam suddenly felt the urge to purchase a fleet of vehicles for all the priests in the city.[243]

Turf

ATHLETIC CLUB

August 30, 1950

Mr. John H. Deavours
Chamber of Commerce
Houston, Texas

Dear Mr. Deavours:

As a means of expressing our gratitude for your most
valued friendship, we are cordially inviting you to
celebrate your birthday, Wednesday, September 6th, in
the Balinese Room.

This invitation, which includes a birthday cake and
dinner for two, compliments of the Turf Athletic Club,
is sent with our sincere wishes for many more years of
good health and happiness.

We are looking forward to your note of acceptance, and
further, your advising whether you desire additional
reservations for friends and members of your family.

Please state your preference for either the dinner period
which begins at 6 p.m., or the supper period which com-
mences at 10 p.m.

Sincerely,

Sam Maceo

SM:g
    j
    t

On the Beach · **BALINESE ROOM**
Telephone 2-8421
Downtown Clubrooms · STUDIO LOUNGE
Telephone 3-2311
General Offices 2214 MARKET ST., GALVESTON, TEX.

Letter from Sam Maceo to John Deavours, dated August 30, 1950. *Anonymous private collection.*

The family's ultimate charitable contribution came in 1947 when Sam Maceo organized a fundraiser for the relief fund for victims of the Texas City Disaster of 1947, an industrial explosion that killed nearly six hundred people and injured more than five thousand. Sam rallied the nation's most famous celebrities for a benefit show held at the Galveston City Auditorium (now demolished). If all of the talent who donated their time at Sam's request had been paid, it would have tallied more than $2 million. Frank Sinatra made a brief appearance, but the star-studded performance highlighted singer and up-and-coming Hollywood star Doris Day, whose blue eyes and sweet demeanor captivated the crowd, and the lightning-fast wit of Bob Hope, whose antics were met with riotous laughter that thundered through the crowded auditorium. Hope and Day followed their acts with an encore at the Balinese Room. Toward the end of the evening, long after Doris Day sang her reprise, Bob Hope was invited up to say a few words. "I thought you would have asked me sooner," he quipped. "For a while I thought I would have to pay for my dinner."[244]

The private lives of Sam and Rose reflected the two sides of their public careers, both the perilous and the peaceful. Sam divorced his first wife, Jessica McBride, in 1941 but not before he sold his interests in the family businesses for $40,000, of which Jessica received half, to elude not only greater losses in the divorce proceedings but also court scrutinization of his financial records. After the split was finalized, he repurchased his shares. Soon after, Sam met ballet dancer and minor Hollywood actress Edna Marie Sedgwick, who came to Galveston with a performance troupe. The couple was married on March 26, 1942, in California. Sam was a doting father to their twin sons, Salvatore Jr. and Edward, born on August 18, 1942, and their daughter, Sedgie, born exactly two years later, on the twins' second birthday. Every year, Sam hosted a gala birthday celebration in their honor.

Rose married Frances Dispensa in 1922 after the untimely death of his first wife, Minnie, and the two lived quietly together until 1951 when they adopted a son, Rosario Jr. The eldest Maceo brother was fiercely protective of his wife, especially after their house at 2412 Avenue O was burglarized in 1950. He installed floodlights around the perimeter of his house that shone all night long and sometimes accompanied them with armed guards.[245]

Despite the precarious nature of their lifestyles, or perhaps because of it, Sam and Rose "were not strutting hoodlums with their well-tailored jackets bulging over holsters."[246] They were gentlemen and upstanding citizens, no matter where the line of legality was drawn, and they worked

INDEX TO MARRIAGES

When Recorded			WOMEN MARRIED		TO WHOM MARRIED		Where Recorded	
Year	Month	Day					Book	Page
1942	Jan	2	Searle	Marguerite L	William R Bergren		1775	31
		5	Sera	Mary	Andrew V Gallego		"	263
		7	Searfoss	Phyllis J	Harry L Ellenburg		1776	229
		8	Seggerman	Dorothy	Dale W Dorr		"	257
		13	Serveny	Ann M	Raymond E Crandall Jr		1777	277
		"	Selis	Florence B C	George A Prosser		"	278
		20	Seeley	Myrtle B	John J Michel		1779	113
		"	Senator	Hazel	William M Wilson		"	114
		21	Searl	Mabel A	Frederic McL Bruderlin		"	171
		27	Sewell	Lucille B	Edward W Hardy		1780	286
		28	Sellers	Lela	William B Mitchell		1781	69
		29	Seling	Irene D	William A Havens Jr		"	144
Feb	2		Serdenthal	Dorothy M	Robert D Sirey		1782	43
		3	Seefeld	Mathilda	Charles F Hunt		"	189
		"	Serracino	Florence	Lanny J Packard		"	190
		"	Seyforth	Doris M	Orville J Dougherty		"	191
		4	Sennett	Ruth C	Oliver I Reiser		1783	14
		6	Seyster	Marion E	Harry W Scott		"	150
		9	Seitzinger	Maxine M	Royce H Gramm		1784	76
		10	Seiff	Julia	Karle H Karpe		"	174
		16	Segner	Jean E	Joseph M Sundeen		1785	226
		"	Seton	Marilyn V	Frank J Ziegler Jr		"	227
		17	Searle	Lillian Y	Walter L Rasmussen		1786	212
		"	Seigel	Marion	Joseph S Debney		"	213
		18	Sesti	Esther M	Henry W Dionysius Jr		1787	108
		"	Seaton	Hazel L	Raymond A Treydte		"	109
		19	Seidel	Helen M	Roy D Kemsley		"	213
		21	Seiler	Elizabeth L	James A Dalton		1788	209
		"	Sellores	Shirlee Y	David H Stewart		"	210
		25	Sekiguchi	Hazue	Sadahei Oishi		1789	26
Mar	3		Seastrom	Florence F	George F Backus		1790	66
		"	Selecman	Louise A	James R Nichols		"	67
		5	Semel	Muriel D	Joseph H Lipour		"	191
		7	Seal	Frances H	John Murmalo		"	261
		9	Seager	Gloria H	James Viti		1791	62
		"	Sechinger	Ethel L	Harold A Holston		"	63
		19	Sexton	Patricia E	Carleton B Cromie		1793	53
		26	Sedgwick	Edna M	Salvatore Maceo		1794	252
		31	Seland	Betty	Gerald Gustad		1795	264
Apr	1		Sedwick	Evelyn R	John L Bygren		1796	31

Index of marriages listing Sam Maceo and Edna Sedgwick. *Ancestry.com.*

endlessly to overcome the liabilities of their chosen profession and prove themselves a benefit to Galveston.

On the municipal front, the Maceos were dedicated civic leaders, members of the Rotary and Lions Clubs and sponsors of every movement that sought to enhance the good life in Galveston. They kept organized crime out of the city and violent crime off the streets.[247] The recorded crime rate was

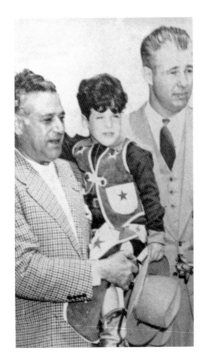

Sam Maceo holding a young boy, possibly one of his sons. *Rosenberg Library.*

the lowest it had ever been on the island, often attributed to the Maccos' personal police force. The crew is often referred to historically as Rose's Night Riders, but that name is an altogether unfair portrayal. Unlike the violent vigilantes who originated the name, the Maceos' crew was a security service, not a hitman or extortion operation. The Maceos were moving loads of money around the island with the ever-present possibility that they could be robbed. The force was assembled to protect the slot machines, clubs and currency, but their presence undoubtedly curtailed a myriad of other street crimes.[248] Local law enforcement had little more to do than handle the drunks and keep the peace.

Sam and Rose were personal friends and campaign donors of the various mayors and city commissioners who served during their time. Envelopes of cash would often find their way to Austin when a friend launched a new campaign at the state level.[249] This was a group within which they found one of their closest allies, Mayor Herbert "Thanks a Million" Cartwright. At thirty-two years of age, Cartwright was the youngest man ever elected to Galveston's highest position, and he retained it for an unprecedented five terms. Affable, intelligent and outspoken, he greeted every resident, from dockhand to businessman, with the same warmth and appreciation.

Cartwright had also dismantled the Sealy-Kempner control of the Galveston wharves even before he was elected mayor, revealing that the families were "stealing people blind." His pal W.L. Moody Jr. provided the collateral for the city's purchase of the wharves, possibly because he presumed that the city would default, but due to added activity from World War II, it did not. Cartwright's intervention led to years of Galveston having the only profitable municipally owned wharves in the country, although that status has significantly faltered in modern times. As far as the Maceos were concerned, Herbie admitted to being on one end of a veritable "hotline" that fed from Austin to Galveston. When anyone in the state government

Sam Maceo posing with Mayor Herbert Cartwright (*far right*). *Rosenberg Library*.

The construction of the original Pleasure Pier at Twenty-Fifth and Seawall. *Rosenberg Library.*

started to draw attention to the wide-open city of sin, the mayor would receive a call that alerted him to their impending visit.[250]

In 1945, Sam Maceo and W.L. Moody Jr. decided that Seawall Boulevard would be safer and more attractive if it were brilliantly illuminated. They pledged funds and took the idea to the chamber of commerce, where it was approved and passed along to the convention department for execution. After a year of fundraising, the innovative $100,000 project ($1.3 million today) broke ground on November 12, 1946, and took two years to complete. When it was finished, 139 blazing lights along the Boulevard created the "Great White Way of Galveston."[251] Around this time, Maceo and Moody also teamed up to assist the city by assuming control of the original Pleasure Pier.

In 1944, while Fort Crockett and Fort Jacinto teemed with active World War II military men, Galveston erected a $1 million Municipal Pleasure Pier that jettisoned 1,130 feet over the Gulf at the foot of Twenty-Fifth Street. Initiated as a recreation center for servicemen but also open to the public, the pier and its windowless metal ballroom was a disastrous failure. It closed the same summer that it opened and remained vacant and untouched for two years. Maceo, Moody and W.H. Autrey took over the city-chartered corporation, signed a ten-year lease and invested $200,000 in improvements. The ballroom was air-conditioned, given the Maceo

This postcard of the Pleasure Pier (*foreground*) also shows the extended pier and T-head of the Balinese at the top of the artist rendering. *Rosenberg Library*.

touch and renamed the Marine Room. An aquarium was installed, along with a 36,000-square-foot exhibition hall, and a 1,500-seat amphitheater was constructed at the end of the pier. A Galveston history museum with relics from the Civil War and the island's original inhabitants, the Karankawa tribe, completed the spectacle. The Pleasure Pier reopened on May 29, 1948.[252]

The Maceos had banked with the Moodys for years and were permitted to borrow hundreds of thousands of dollars with nothing but a stroke of the pen. The loan was usually repaid in two weeks with generous interest. At times when W.L. Moody III was on the outs with his father, he could count on the Maceos to lend him the $150,000 for an investment of which Junior disapproved. The Moodys and the Maceos even shared the same lawyer, Louis Dibrell, but the relationship encountered turbulence in the mid-1930s when Sam Maceo auspiciously lamented the deficiency of high-end accommodations for his elite club patrons and remarked that Moody's hotels lacked style and luxury. Moody Jr. was already sensitive about his hotels; he was rumored to have disowned his son because he installed air-conditioning at the Jack Tar (now demolished). Moody did not want to have to incur that expense at the Buccaneer, but without it the hotel would seem outdated in comparison.

Beach scene with the original Pleasure Pier. *Rosenberg Library.*

When the Maceos decided to remodel the Snug Harbor Hotel at Twenty-Third and Avenue Q into upscale apartments for short-term rentals, Moody Jr. summoned Rose and told him plainly, "I have stayed out of the gambling business, and I expect you to stay out of the hotel business."[253] This unceremonious treatment (as it was perceived by Moody) seemed to stick with the hotelier, and he was widely thought to have been the one who hired the prostitute to plant the narcotics in Sam's car that led to his 1937 arrest. However, Moody Jr. was eventually forced to shelve his grudge, if one existed, when the Maceos presented him with an opportunity that surpassed even that of his own island dynasty.

10
WHAT HAPPENED IN VEGAS

W.L. Moody Jr. had done well with the fortune bequeathed from his father, Colonel W.L. Moody, an attorney who first opened a mercantile trading company in Fairfield, Texas, before moving to Galveston in 1866. The Civil War colonel started in the cotton trading business in the 1870s and became an integral player in the advancement of the Port of Galveston. He worked to bring railroad lines to the island, championed the dredging and deepening of the harbor to allow for larger vessels and was the first to build a dockside cotton compress. Moody Jr. established the American National Insurance Company (ANICO) in 1905 and founded Moody Bank with his father in 1908. In 1945, a vivacious eighty-year-old Moody Jr. was the hands-on owner and operator of the only private bank in the country, countless hotels, cattle ranches, newspapers and, of course, ANICO and the cotton enterprises. He did not socialize with the Maceos, although he rarely socialized with anyone and greatly preferred working late at the office to donning a tuxedo to patronize Sam's nightclub.[254] Junior did, however, consider the Maceos friends and never hesitated to engage with them professionally.

Concurrently, a mirage on the deserts sands of Nevada had appeared to Bugsy Siegel, the former New York Mafia hitman who moved to Los Angeles in 1936 and became head of the West Coast Mafia syndicate. The state legalized gambling in 1931 as a drastic response to a crumbling economy and fleeing population, but Reno was the only city that had capitalized on the industry to any notable degree. The setting of Siegel's vision was four hundred miles to the northwest on the arid, dusty and near-vacant desert plains of Las Vegas. He conjured images of a gambling oasis suffused with luxury and grandeur, but he knew that it would take more than games of chance. "His lure, in addition to the tables, would be the best food, the best accommodations and the greatest entertainers, all at such low prices that no high roller could afford to stay away."[255] Sounds familiar.

Siegel's enthusiasm garnered the support of fellow syndicate bosses from around the country, and once the mob's famed financial genius Meyer Lansky endorsed the idea, investments rolled in from every region of the underworld. The initial budget for Siegel's flagship Flamingo was $1.5 million, but that did not account for his exorbitant quality standards or his mistress, who was given free rein of the interior design allotments and, over time, siphoned off millions into foreign accounts. Siegel repeatedly returned to Lansky and other dons for more money. They always complied, but with each request, the investors grew increasingly apprehensive. Siegel was not invited to the 1946 Havana Conference where prominent leaders of various syndicates called for his elimination. However, Bugsy was acutely aware of the strain that the Flamingo was having on his relationship with the organization, and he finally announced that their ships would come in on December 26, 1946.[256]

The $6 million Flamingo was a flop, and the failure of opening night was exacerbated by revelations of his mistress's financial indiscretions. The invested mafioso ordered Siegel's execution, but the potential of his Vegas vision was undeniable, so he was granted a stay to prove that the dream was achievable. History has proven that it was, but Siegel never lived to see it. Though he seemed to reach his watershed moment when the club registered a $300,000 gross in May 1947, at 10:45 p.m. on June 20, 1947, a fusillade from a .30-caliber carbine exploded through the living room window of Siegel's rented Beverly Hills mansion where he sat reading a newspaper. One bullet ripped through his head, and four more struck his torso. As he bled out on the couch, three Lansky associates walked into a Las Vegas lobby and proclaimed that they were taking over the Flamingo.[257] Bugsy Siegel's vast and intricate network of syndicate stakeholders had eliminated their middleman, and Vegas belonged to the Mafia and Meyer Lansky.

One seeming exception on Vegas's early roster was Wilbur Clark, a Reno craps dealer who was purported to be a "clean" gambler, free of any Mafia connections.[258] In 1947, Clark and his brother secured $250,000 and broke ground on Wilbur Clark's Desert Inn at 3145 Las Vegas Boulevard South, between Desert Inn Road and Sands Avenue. They ran out of money almost immediately, and the partially finished structure baked in a desert oven for

Sam Maceo was in the constant company of A-listers. Here he is pictured with screen star Marjorie Reynolds (*far left*). *Rosenberg Library.*

From left to right: Alice Faye, Phil Harris, Marjorie Reynolds and Jack Benny with Maceo children outside the Balinese Room, 1947. *Rosenberg Library.*

nearly two years. Clark brought the plight of the Desert Inn to the attention of Moe Dalitz in 1949, and the Cleveland boss offered a $1.3 million investment for a 75 percent silent stake.[259] Soon, Dalitz was on the horn to recruit his old rumrunning accomplice, Sam Maceo.

Dalitz and Maceo had formed their partnership when Moe's routes across Lake Erie from Canada were thwarted by authorities. Seeking a new path through the Gulf of Mexico, Dalitz allied with the Maceos to divert his Canadian shipments through the Caribbean and over to Galveston where they would be sent to Cleveland via railroad.[260] By the 1940s, Sam and Rose had a roster of first-class friends—they knew every oilman in Texas. They had the capital, the know-how and the network to attract both high-end clientele and investors. Dalitz offered the Maceos a 30 percent stake of the Desert Inn, knowing that Sam's involvement would be beneficial on all levels—aesthetic, financial and political.[261] He was correct.

Are You Sure This Is Texas?

The Maceos were ready for Las Vegas. The ambiance they established in Galveston was so glamorous it made many people ask, "Are you sure this is Texas?" as portrayed in this comic. Galveston Isle *magazine, Rosenberg Library*.

Sam Maceo with comedian Jack Benny (*right*). The picture was taken just after Sam pranked the famous comedian by having the waiter present him the check. *Rosenberg Library.*

Despite not being in the operational forefront of the casino, Dalitz's partnership would still require a gaming license, a request promptly rejected by the Nevada Gaming Commission because of past convictions. Sam scheduled a meeting with United States senator from Nevada Pat McCarran on Moe's behalf. The unshakable, infinitely likeable Galveston diplomat conversed and dined with the senator at his regular table inside the Riverside Hotel and Casino in Reno for three hours. What exactly transpired at that meeting is unknown, but Dalitz was immediately granted the license that just days before had been denied.[262] Likely, Maceo brought more to the table than a steady hand of persuasion. McCarran and Maceo had a mutual friend in W.L. Moody Jr., and Moe's million-dollar investment in the Desert Inn was being financed by ANICO.[263]

The 2,400-square-foot Desert Inn was the largest casino in Vegas when it was built. It was situated on 170 acres that included an eighteen-hole golf course, a spa, a gourmet restaurant, sprawling outdoor verandas, a 450-seat dinner theater, a rooftop lounge and a variety of specialty shops. Undoubtedly touched by the Maceo magic, the Desert Inn was especially lauded for its effortless elegance and first-rate service. Invitations for the grand debut were sent out to a list of 150 top-tier VIPs, offering a $10,000 credit limit for their gaming enjoyment. The two-day opening celebration commenced on April 24, 1950, and the owners paid the airfare for journalists from the nation's major publications to ensure their attendance. Reporters swarmed around a slate of prominent Hollywood figures, including Bud Abbott and Lou Costello, while Sam stood in the background, jubilant but unnoticed.[264]

The Maceos were soon in talks with Jake Friedman, the eccentric Houstonian who had sold them his percentage of the Hollywood Dinner Club. Friedman was cultivating capital for a new casino complex called the Sands, and the Maceos were again invested for 30 percent.[265] The list of investors was extensive and included Meyer Lansky and Frank Costello, head of New York's Luciano syndicate, while 9 percent was owned by Frank Sinatra.[266] Meanwhile, the Maceos were planning to move the whole family to Las Vegas. Since the Desert Inn, Sam and Rose had been grooming their nephews Frank, Victor and Anthony Fertitta for mid-level club management to take over the front-of-house positions as they transitioned their attention to a location where their far-reaching ideas would no longer be overshadowed by illegality. Vic and Anthony, sons of Sam and Rose's sister Olivia Maceo Fertitta, balanced each other well, just like their uncles. Anthony was the front man and manager of the Balinese dining room, and Vic oversaw the casino. Their sister Olivia Fertitta (1916–1955) married one of the Balinese Room's star dealers, Loranzy (Lorenzo) Grilliette, in 1936.[267] Grilliette was promoted to co-manager of the Studio Lounge with Anthony after its remodel, and he took over as sole manager when Anthony was transferred to the Balinese.[268] He later moved to Las Vegas and was a pit boss and upper-level management at Friedman's Sands for several years.[269]

In 1951, a genteel southern senator in horn-rimmed glasses exposed the nation's underbelly to a captivated American audience. Tennessean Estes T. Kefauver, chair of the U.S. Senate Committee to Investigate Crime and Interstate Commerce, organized a nationwide round-up of mobsters, corrupt politicians and bribe-happy lawmen. Historically remembered as the Kefauver Committee, it did more than produce perspiration on the brows of nervous, finger-strumming mobsters—it introduced them to the world. The hearings were aired on television and radio stations across the country, and Americans were exposed to the inner workings of organized crime for the first time, amid an already skittish postwar climate of nuclear and Communist conspiracies. An estimated nine out of ten television sets in the United States were continually tuned to the broadcast. No one from

Aboard the TAC yacht *Rainbow* are Frank Maceo (*far left*) and Edna Sedgwick Maceo (*front*), as well as Anthony Fertitta (*back row, second from right*) and Lorenzo Grilliette (*far right*). *Rosenberg Library.*

the Maceo outfit was included in the debacle, but in Texas, the hearings sparked the imagination of an enterprising state attorney general named Price Daniel who had his eye on the governor's seat. Within months, Daniel launched a state investigation into the Maceo enterprises, often referred to as the Little Kefauver hearings. Texas Rangers served subpoenas to six members of the Galveston empire, but only five of them appeared.

Sam Maceo died at 5:30 p.m. on April 16, 1951, at Johns Hopkins Hospital in Baltimore. He had been ailing for some time and was admitted on March 28 for an operation on his esophagus, but after a brief rally, he was reported to have succumbed to complications from the surgery.[270] The cause of death, however, was listed as cancer of the digestive tract. Five days prior to Sam's death and nine days after he was called to testify before the Kefauver Committee, Chicago mobster and ex-Capone bodyguard Charlie Fischetti died of a heart attack. Fischetti had attended the 1946 combine in Havana and was given the contract on Bugsy Siegel. On April 19, the body of Phil Mangano, a member of New York's Gambino crime

EDITOR'S NOTE: *Sam Maceo invisioned a magazine that would be dedicated to one of his first loves—Galveston.* GALVESTON ISLE, *which was first published in July, 1947, was that dream come true. Off the record, this was his pet project or endeavor. It was through his efforts that* GALVESTON ISLE *was created and maintained. As our publisher and boss Sam Maceo will always be remembered in the hearts of members of the* GALVESTON ISLE *staff. We loved him—and he was the best friend we have ever known. May God bless him and may he forever rest in peace.*

Galveston Isle magazine ran a touching tribute to its publisher, Sam Maceo, after his death. *Rosenberg Library.*

family, was found in the marshes of Sheepshead Bay, Brooklyn—the same day that his brother Vincent, head of the Gambinos, vanished entirely. Vincent's body was never found. The brothers had also been called to testify, and both were at odds with Vincent's underboss Albert Anastasia, an ally of Sands investor Frank Costello. To the more sophisticated federal agents, the fact that these consecutive deaths were simultaneously linked both to investigative hearings and to Las Vegas seemed like much more than a coincidence.[271]

After Sam's passing, Rose brought everyone in Vegas back to Galveston, which could hint that he suspected a connection between his brother's sudden death and his introduction to Northeast and Midwest syndicate

The right half of this famous panorama from the Balinese Room has never before been published. The family gathered to celebrate Rose's birthday shortly after Sam passed away. *Family collection.*

leaders through his work in Nevada. However, the allure of Vegas had been the legality, and the Maceos had already gone legal in most of their Galveston enterprises. They had extensive oil, gas and real estate holdings, and they also loved the island.[272] When pondering the move, Gigolo Maceo shrugged and said frankly, "I can't leave Galveston!"[273]

Their love of the island was reciprocated, and Sam's passing was an outright tragedy to the thousands who knew and loved him. He was remembered not as an outlaw, but as a businessman whose success never erased the memories of the meager days in Leesville when he worked in sawmills and furniture shops with his father, for whom merely feeding and clothing his family were perpetual struggles. Publicly, Sam was poised, polished and larger than life, but privately, he was a humble benefactor who never drew attention to his philanthropic efforts, which ranged from hosting an annual city-wide Christmas party for local kids to establishing a blood bank at St. Mary's Infirmary.

Even in death, he gave of himself, requesting that money be donated to a cause rather than used to buy flowers for his grave. The Galveston County chapter of the American Cancer Society received nearly $3,000 in memorial gifts, and another local charity fund received twice that. For the city of Galveston and future generations, Sam left behind an architectural masterpiece within the confines of the Cedar Lawn subdivision. Although it was not completed until after his death, the breathtaking domicile seemed to be his soul incarnate, epitomizing a glamorous subset of the mid-century modern architectural movement known as desert-modernism. It was designed by E. Stewart Williams of Palm Springs, California, who also designed Frank Sinatra's Twin Palms; 43 Cedar Lawn Circle was his only work in the greater Houston area. At Sam's funeral, retired reverend Monsignor Daniel P. O'Connell cited the frailties of human nature and said of him, "Charity covers a multitude of sins."[274]

Although the Maceos had pulled out of Vegas, the ANICO money stuck around. Colonel W.L. Moody Jr. died in July 1954, and a bitter feud erupted among his scions when they learned that he left his entire estate to the Moody Foundation. For fifteen years, family members vied for control and attempted to wrestle income from the embroiled estate. Several lawsuits were filed, and investigations were initiated. Moody's son Shearn financed an investigator named Norman D. Revie, who was most persistent and spent two years looking into the books of American National. He searched courthouses from twelve different states and collected thousands of documents. In 1971, a Texas legislative committee initiated its own investigation and revealed that even as the nation's tenth-largest insurer, ANICO's chief undertaking during the 1950s and '60s was lending money to Las Vegas interests via known mafioso. Family members claimed that they knew nothing of these activities until they were revealed in 1969. Two of ANICO's top officers, William L. Vogler and Rollins A. Furbush, took the rap and were fully credited with initiating the casino loans, but they had both worked for W.L. Moody Jr. starting in the early 1940s.[275]

Vogler and Furbush also allegedly created a dummy corporation, sold it to ANICO for an inflated $3 million and used the money to become part-owners of Leonard J. Campbell Enterprises, a Vegas company with contractual rights to the Dunes Hotel and Casino. Another Dunes affiliate was Morris Shenker, described by *Life* magazine as the "foremost lawyer for the mob in the United States." Shenker brokered the sale of the dummy corporation and put together another deal that loaned $1.8 million to the M&R Investment Company for their investment in the Dunes. Over five years, ANICO loaned $13.2 million to Shenker, and an ensuing multitude of vested Vegas mobsters graciously welcomed the alternative capital after years of using their personal money. ANICO loans and investments originating in Vegas included $5.3 million to the Thunderbird Hotel and Casino, $3.6 million to the Riviera Hotel and Casino, $1.5 million to Circus Circus, $4 million to Sahara and Mint, $3.3 million to Sahara Tahoe and Casino at Reno, $6 million to Harrah's, $1.5 million to the Flamingo and $2.5 million to the Sands. Within a four-year period starting in 1967, ANICO invested $31.75 million in Nevada casinos.[276] Between a concept invented by the Maceos and the cash provided by American National, that rambling desert metropolis, the nation's gaudy and glittering playground, owes its very existence to the original sin city. Long live Las Vegas—the city that Galveston built.

11

SHUTTERED

Less than two months after Sam died, Rose Maceo, Sam Serio and Vic Fertitta answered the summons to appear before the house crime investigating committee in Austin. They were accompanied by their office manager, R.H. Cox, and their cousin Frank, the third-largest investor in the Maceo empire and manager of the bookmaking operation at the TAC.[277] The only one of the five granted immunity was Sam "Books" Serio, and unsurprisingly, he was the only one who responded to questions with anything more than "I refuse to answer." His testimony still did not reveal much of consequence, and he ended with an emphatic declaration that the Maceo businesses were "closed for good."[278] Gigolo Maceo was also called to testify, although he was not charged. The entire hearing was broadcast live on the radio in Galveston, echoing out of every barbershop and diner in town.[279]

Homer Garrison, chief of the Texas Department of Public Safety, testified to the committee, "There's nothing you can do about gambling in the Balinese or in Galveston because the juries simply won't convict a man for gambling down there."[280] Sheriff Frank Biaggne of Galveston County was asked why he never raided the Balinese. "I went to the door several times," he answered, "but they wouldn't let me in because I was not a member. I'd say, 'How about getting in?' but the man on the door would say 'Nothing doing,' so I'd walk away."[281] A grand jury handed down twenty-three indictments because of Price Daniel's investigative committee, but the family attorney Louis Dibrell was granted a continuance five times. After more than a year of these postponements, ten of the indictments were dismissed by Galveston County district judge Donald Markle, and the remainder were thrown out by Judge Charles G. Dibrell. The Balinese and all Maceo operations did close after the hearings but only until the lurking Texas Rangers were called away to Port Arthur a few days later.[282]

When Rose returned to Galveston, he sank into a deep depression. In preparation for the future, he and his brother had internally restructured the Galveston business in late 1950. Under Turf Athletic Club, Sam and Rose each had a 20 percent stake, Frank and A.J. Adams each had 15 percent, Dutch Voight and Vic C. retained 10 percent each and Sam Serio and Vincent Maceo owned 5 percent. In October 1950, Sam, Rose, Dutch and Vic C. each gave up 5 percent, Frank gave up 7½ percent and Adams gave up 10 percent. The name of the parent company was changed to Maceo and Company, and the 37½ percent relinquished by the older Maceos was sold to several "junior" Maceos, including nephews Gigolo Maceo, Anthony, Vic and Frank Fertitta, as well as their cousin Little Sammie and Lorenzo Grilliette.[283] Sam's shares were put into a trust after his death, while the younger Maceos continued their management of the clubs. Rose maintained his position as overseer of Maceo and Company, but his work was overshadowed with mourning for both his brother and the writing on the wall. When Serio announced at Little Kefauver that they were closed for good to elude further investigation, everyone except the people in the courtroom believed him. One Houston newspaper printed "Galveston is Closed!" in huge letters across the top of the front page.[284] The clubs reopened, but the difference was palpable.

With the velvet glove gone, the iron glove had lost his match, and a sinking empire intensified the loss. Rose died of heart failure—or heartbreak—on March 29, 1954. Besides one barely believable story of a man who was shot on the Seawall after robbing the Sui Jen and somehow managed to hang on just long enough to whisper, "It was Rose!" to a responding officer,[285] the only tale used to demonstrate the abundant theory of Rose as the ferocious enforcer has been the wholly false narrative about his first wife's death. Even the secondhand naming of their security force as Rose's Night Riders had misguided connotations. Undoubtedly, the reputation was useful, and his mysterious and quiet demeanor did nothing to confirm or deny the rumors, thus the gossips chose to believe what they chose to believe, and Rose chose to let them believe it. He did not rule by fear; he ruled with cunning, genius and a graceful ability to command respect without saying a word.

REGISTRATION CARD—(Men born on or after April 28, 1877 and on or before February 16, 1897)

World War II draft card for Rose Maceo lists him as an owner of the Turf Athletic Club. *Ancestry.com.*

The two murders within the Maceos' nearly forty-year reign, one of which contained only miniscule traces of their involvement, were intentional, calculated and precisely directed at protecting their city from detrimental outside influence. Galveston was not the scene of a St. Valentine's Day Massacre or a rocket launcher blasting through a living room window because someone owed the family money. The extent of the Maceos' habitually repeated offenses were breaking laws that they proved, contrary to widespread opinion, as utterly unnecessary for a peaceful, functioning society.

Six months after Rose's death, a fire broke out at the Balinese Room. Extensive damage was done to the interior, and Sophie Tucker, who had sent seven large trunks in advance of her scheduled two-week engagement, lost everything but a few mementos. The trunks contained several gowns totaling tens of thousands of dollars, but she was incredibly gracious. "Don't let a fire make your spirits low," she said to Vic and Anthony. "You have the know-how and the admiration of the entertainment business. Build a new Balinese Room, and I promise to come back and open it for you."[286] The rebuild cost more than $750,000, two-thirds of which was spent on the interior alone.[287] The Balinese served more than seven hundred people each night of the

Photograph taken inside Murdoch's pier of Rose Maceo seated in front of (*right to left*) Anthony Fertitta, Sheriff Frank Biaggne and Constable "Rabbit" Feigle.

grand-reopening weekend. Sophie Tucker performed as she had promised, but misfortune seemed to follow her to Galveston. In the middle of one of her performances, she took ill and was rushed to the hospital.[288]

Often uncredited, Frank Maceo succeeded his cousins Sam and Rose as head of the empire.[289] Vic and Anthony Fertitta are almost always named by history as the successors, seemingly as an assumed overinflation of the fact that they managed the Balinese Room. They were strictly mid-level management, but their positions at Galveston's most famous club put them in the spotlight, as did their youth, inexperience and volatility. In July 1955, an undercover reporter and his photographer went to Galveston and entered the sports-betting parlor of the TAC. They were exposed only after obtaining all the evidence they needed, but Vic and Anthony tracked them to the Hotel Galvez, where the journalists had recently arrived to turn in for the night. The photographer got away and rushed up to the room with the photos, but the reporter was not as fortunate. Anthony punched him and knocked him down; the severity of the blow depends on which side tells the story. Regardless, these two were not rag-beat tabloid employees, they were journalists for *Life* magazine—reporter Henry Suydam Jr. and photographer Joe Scherschel. The next issue of *Life* released on August 15, 1955, featured an exposé titled "Wide-Open Galveston Mocks Texas Laws." The brief but scathing article ridiculed Galveston and state officials and included an account of the attack, as well as photos of Suydam's blackened cheekbone, a dice table at the Rio Grande and the interior of TAC's back room.[290] In one day, Galveston went from the quirky black sheep of Texas and the playground of the South to national pariah.

The visit of Suydam and Scherschel, however mishandled, was instigated by Galveston's election of Mayor Roy Clough over incumbent Herbert Cartwright. With the best of intentions, Clough declared Galveston an "open, clean town," clean meaning discreet, no rigged gambling devices and no soliciting. Clough protested that vice was always going to exist, so it might as well be regulated.[291] In this vein, he also argued that a closed town led to corruption among city officials, pointing to the city's police commissioner, Walter Johnston, who had allegedly used payoffs from local vice dens to enrich himself to the sum of $40,000.[292] Clough's forward-thinking philosophy was mishandled by national media outlets and came off as utterly absurd to people outside of Galveston, and he responded by writing his own op-ed to explain his stance.[293] This was met with even more ridicule, and magazines declared Galveston a "wide-open sin town."[294] If nothing else, the Maceos' success was contingent upon their discretion. They did not flaunt or promote gambling; it was not the first thing a guest saw when they walked into a club, and it was not forced on anyone. Neither did they spend time trying to justify their business model. Galveston was insulated by the premise that it did not need or care for outside approval, and Clough's quest for it undermined the very foundation of the empire.

The Maceo Empire faltered further when Frank, Vic C., Sam Serio and Sam Maceo's widow, Edna, were charged with tax evasion in December 1955 for three reporting years between 1948 and 1950. A.J. Adams, listed as the vice president of Gulf Properties, also had a case pending against him. The charges themselves were not as troublesome as the exposure of their internal financial documents that revealed profits of $3 million in each of the years called into question, as well as a jewelry purchase topping $100,000 and a story about $600,000 in cash taken out of a concealed safe.[295] In comparison, Al Capone was pulling in an estimated $100 million per year in his heyday, but the Maceo numbers were still alarming to some Galveston

Famous golfer Jimmie Demaret (*left*) with Anthony Fertitta. *Rosenberg Library*.

residents whose only basis for comparison was their monthly wage. The island's empirical rock was quickly transforming into sinking sand.

Even as these events transpired, state officials seemed to take little notice, or if they did, they took no action until well-meaning Galvestonians made the inadvertent mistake of asking for help from the wrong person. The day Rose died, Sheriff Biaggne showed up at the TAC building demanding a payoff—a bold move but indicative of the strength of Rose's reputation. The Maceos apparently complied because he continued his harassment. Their money did nothing to satiate the sheriff's newfound greed, however, and he began extending his racket to local business owners who kept slot machines, threatening to close them down if he was not paid. In casual conversation, at least one Maceo bemoaned the situation to their influential friends who were directly benefiting from their enterprises. The friends decided to intervene by calling Texas assistant attorney general Will Wilson and asking him to rein in Biaggne.[296]

The ambitious Wilson fielded the complaint with vague iterations of support, but instead of complying with their request, he realized that the information now in his possession was his ticket to the governor's seat. Price Daniel's efforts netted scant results—only five clubs in Galveston were closed for fewer days—but the next year, he was elected to the highest office in the state. Since then, the incredulity brought on by the Kefauver hearings both big and little had continued to percolate, and the Maceos were undoubtedly viewed as suspect by the rest of Texas. Only Galvestonians were privy to the upstanding elements that dominated the Maceo operation, while the rest of the state was given the government's side of the story and therefore assumed that the Maceos were exactly like the hardened criminals of the Kefauver broadcasts.

This was a distinct advantage to Wilson. He figured that if he could outdo Daniel even to the slightest degree, his future was all but guaranteed.[297] First, Wilson would need the means to execute his plan freely, and his assistant position was sorely lacking the autonomy required for him to receive the credit for his scheme. In 1956, Will Wilson was victorious in his bid for attorney general. His campaign was based almost exclusively on a platform of ridding Texas of the evils and ills of vice. He thought himself quite clever for suggesting that Galveston exchange its underground economy for the whimsy of a family-friendly beach town,[298] but islanders heartily rejected his view. They had fame and fortune, style and sophistication, mystery and intrigue, and they were not interested in sandy feet and picnic baskets.

Wilson had no ethical misgivings about the goings-on in Galveston, evidenced by the fact that his only targets were the gambling and the illegal consumption of liquor by the drink—he cared nothing about the island's thriving red-light district on Postoffice Street. "The Line," as it was known, completed the trifecta of island vice and was the preeminent indication of Galveston's alternative societal standards, defined by a disregard for convention and subjective morality that earned it the name "The Free State of Galveston." Prostitution on the island predated and outlived the gambling era, with mass, organized prostitution in the form of a recognized district and the madam-brothel system existing for nearly seventy years.

Beach scene in Galveston in 1950. Galveston Isle *magazine, Rosenberg Library.*

But the existence was a tumultuous one. Living outside the law without the protection of wealth or social standing made the women of the Line susceptible to unending harassment from politicians, police and sheriffs who would defend the industry publicly by saying it was a "biological necessity"[299] and then turn around and exploit it for their own personal profit. Much of Commissioner Johnston's $40,000 windfall came from the red-light district.

At the start of his term, Will Wilson told Galveston officials that he would give them six months to clean it up on their own before he offered his unsolicited assistance. More than an eye roll–worthy token of generosity, the six months were for Wilson to plan his strategy. It also gave the American Social Hygiene Association (ASHA) time to convince Wilson to add prostitution to his moral checklist. The ASHA was a national organization formed in 1914 in response to the "social purity movement." It sought to end prostitution throughout the country. Although its efforts were quite successful in eliminating districts in countless other U.S. cities, the group had been in Galveston for thirteen years, and the red lights still burned as bright as the day they arrived in 1944.

The ASHA took Wilson's assertions at face value and canonized him as its hero. The group made it easy for him to acquiesce to its posturing by saving him the investigatory man-hours. The organization had conducted frequent, routine undercover surveys of prostitution and gambling, and it compiled an up-to-date list of the continuing offenders and their business addresses.[300] All Wilson had to do was add these businesses to his mounting list of potential injunctions that included sixty-five suspected gambling dens, compiled by a covert operative led by George Reed, the chief of intelligence for the region. Wilson's dramatic and publicity-inducing plan was to descend on the island and raid every location on the list simultaneously in one collective demonstration of authority.[301]

Company A of the Texas Rangers, led by Captain Johnny Klevenhagen, scheduled a rendezvous with Reed's team, Will Wilson and a caravan of his assistant attorneys in early June 1957, at the Junior League building on Bissonet Drive in Houston. The Rangers were aware that Wilson had an agenda, but their personal judgments of his attention-seeking were not pertinent to the job at hand. They were to secure search warrants, divide into teams of five—three lawyers and two lawmen per team—and visit every address on the list. The warrants would be presented, and the locations would be raided. Will Wilson gave the Rangers instructions to seize every piece of gambling paraphernalia in the building. Officers Ed Gooding and Pete Rogers were sent to Galveston to get the warrants.[302]

The pair drove to the home of Judge Donald Markle, whose mind flashed back to 1952 while the Rangers stood before him explaining the probable cause that merited his signature on a warrant. Five years prior, Markle dismissed ten indictments against the same family currently in question, but things were different now. If the claims were true that everyone in town was on the Maceo payroll, then Judge Markle's decision would have likely gone another way, or it would have been followed with a phone call to the TAC building. Sam was gone, though, and so was Rose, and it seemed they had taken the prestige with them. The tolerance offered to other club owners in Galveston was based on the effectiveness of Sam and Rose's leadership, but in their absence, the policy was abused. While the state and the nation read sensationalistic articles about "wide-open" Galveston, the door left ajar by the irreplaceable Sam and Rose was slowly starting to shut. A proliferation of gambling halls had suffocated the ambiance of the island and contributed to an increase in violence and shady business practices. The high-budget entertainment went down with the profits. Shootings and crime were again rampant like in the old gangland days.[303] The stories told on the street were those of marked cards and dealers who were not allowed to let anyone win, instead of gossip about the latest Hollywood celebrity in town. No payoff was as valuable as the culture the Maceos created. If money was involved in 1952, it was still there for the taking, but Sam and Rose were not. Judge Markle sighed, and then he took the Ranger's pen.

When Gooding and Rogers returned to the Houston headquarters, Will Wilson had just arrived and was admonishing Captain Klevenhagen, saying that the raids were off because one of his men had leaked information.

Casino chip from the Imperial at 2319 Postoffice, owned by Joe T. Hanson. *Anonymous private collection.*

The captain responded vehemently to the accusations, appalled that the attorney general would even dare suggest that his Rangers were untrustworthy. Wilson quickly retracted his allegation; the only certainty was that the raid was canceled.[304] Fortunately, he had recourse. Upon Wilson's election in late 1956, he had received a letter from an idealistic attorney named Jim Simpson who had moved to Galveston County two years prior and was disgusted with the island's flagrant disrespect of the law. In the letter, Simpson recommended that Wilson use the power of civil injunction in his Galveston efforts, since the office of attorney general could not prosecute criminal cases. Appreciative of Simpson's advice, Wilson appointed him to his office as special assistant attorney general. Simpson hired two undercover civilian operatives, James D. Givens and Carrol Yaws, and over five months, the three amassed a mountain of evidence against Galveston and a list of forty-seven known gambling houses. Unlike the warrant procedure which had proven itself fallible, only four people—Givens, Yaws, Simpson, and Wilson—knew about Simpson's investigation until it concluded on June 1, 1957.[305]

The Texas Rangers called a meeting to devise another scheme the day after the busted raid. This time, they would try patience. Klevenhagen acquired a room on the top floor of Moody's Buccaneer Hotel to keep an ever-present eye on the Balinese Room across the street. As the established queen of Galveston's underground, the eventual demise of the Balinese would be the catalyst for disassembling vice from the top down. The Rangers knew that raids never worked on the Balinese, so they played it slow by seating an officer inside at a table from the time the club opened until the time that it closed. The work was tedious and tiresome for the officers, whose company of eight men patrolled more territory than the island. They planned to work six-week rotations, alternating in and out of Galveston every two weeks and using the remainder to cram six weeks of work from their other jurisdictions into four. It was going to be a grueling, merciless schedule, and worse, the ineffectiveness of the plan was immediately apparent. Their prime-time stakeouts served only to stifle business at the Balinese, did nothing to ensure lasting results and worst of all, the plan's lack of pizazz irritated Wilson.

Klevenhagen called Department of Public Safety chief Homer Garrison and asked for more manpower to engage the original plan of raiding every illicit enterprise on the island simultaneously. Wilson answered that call as well, and a veritable army of lawmen was assembled, including more Texas Rangers and a mass of DPS troopers.[306] Wilson's first scheme had tanked, but the warrants from that effort were still signed. He gave the order and unleashed his forces. They busted down doors and raided every brothel and gambling house on Simpson's list. They even got to the raid-proof Balinese on June 6, 1957.

A former employee who worked in the kitchen of the Balinese Room said that he was prepping for a party of two hundred people when the Rangers busted in the door. "I'm working here!" the cook exclaimed. The ranger quipped back, "You can get a job somewhere else." As he started to leave, a musician came out of a back room with no clothes and told the cook that they

Above: Playing cards were a gift to TAC members, featuring artwork from the Studio Lounge and Balinese Room. *Anonymous private collection.*

Right: The cards were elegantly packaged as a boxed gift set. *Anonymous private collection.*

"beat the hell out of me." Oddly, the alarm had not sounded that night, and the cook surmised from scattered conversations among other employees that they had all been paid off to let the Rangers in unannounced. "Everybody got rich but me and [bandleader] Buddy Kirk," he said.[307]

Unfortunately, the Rangers' earlier slow play had given club owners time to stash their gambling equipment. The establishments were bullied into closing, but seizing the equipment was the surest way for them to stay closed. Without the hard evidence, Wilson was forced to play his ace in the hole. Jim Simpson entered the Galveston County Courthouse on June 10, 1957, and

Rare pepper grinder from the Balinese Room. *Anonymous private collection.*

walked straight to the district clerk's office. He proceeded to file forty-seven civil injunctions. Although lacking showmanship, the grand gesture still managed to get the attention of the statewide press agents who had a riotous time printing bold black headlines of Galveston's demise.[308] Perhaps as a premonition, officials staged a photo shoot at Galveston Novelty, a repair shop where broken machines were scrapped and used for parts. The stunt produced a famous photo where a lawman is callously smashing the face of a slot machine with a large wooden mallet. But the floodgates had opened, and the real equipment started to surface. Around the middle of June, law enforcement discovered 350 slot machines and miscellaneous paraphernalia in an underground bunker at Fort Travis on the Bolivar Peninsula, followed by a cache valued at $800,000 in a bunker at Fort Crockett on the Seawall. The rangers hit the jackpot on June 19, 1957, when the long-forgotten Sixty-First Street Hollywood Dinner Club revealed its secrets.[309]

Inside, they discovered roughly fifteen hundred slot machines, roulette wheels and dice and blackjack tables piled up to the ceiling. Several boxes of dice and casino chips marked "Balinese" were stashed alongside the games. The haul was estimated at $1.2 million. The equipment and six hundred slot machines were loaded into vans and taken to the city dump where they were torched in a fire that could be seen from the mainland. At midnight, the Galveston Fire Department moved in to hose down the smoldering pile of ash and molten metal. Meanwhile, another set of machines had been trucked over to the wharves and loaded onto a tugboat. Rangers managed to squeeze fifty machines on the tiny seagoing vessel, making sure to leave plenty of room onboard for a reporter and his photographer. The gambling equipment was sailed into the harbor and thrown overboard. The next day, the Army Corps of Engineers threatened to charge Wilson and the Texas Rangers with contaminating a waterway, but Will Wilson had gotten his publicity and his results.[310] The lost inventory was a death blow, and Wilson installed one of his assistant attorneys general in an office downtown.[311] The Free State of Galveston was now under lock and key. Or so it seemed.

One year after the raids of 1957, the ASHA conducted another survey of the island. It found that prostitution had not even been reduced by half, and gambling was still rampant, except now it was preying on locals. State officials previously accused Sam and Rose of leeching off their fellow residents, but that did not happen on a large scale until after Wilson's supposed heroics. Furthermore, the raids had done nothing to change people's minds, only their actions. Over the next decade, prostitution and gambling would finally wane, but only because Galveston itself chose to let go. The implications of the 1958 survey troubled the ASHA, and it actively considered suppressing the results in fear that they would hurt Wilson's chance at reelection. In the end, the association quietly released its findings, but they received very little attention.[312] Wilson was reelected two more times but never made it to the governor's seat.

After failed attempts to win both a U.S. Senate seat and the nomination for governor, Wilson seemed destined to remain on the wrong side of history. He changed political affiliations and became a staunch supporter of Richard Nixon. After Nixon's election, the president appointed Wilson to the position of United States attorney general, where he was given front-row access to the commander-in-chief's decline and eventual resignation. Wilson's career

Casino chips from the Balinese Room. *Anonymous private collection.*

ended in a similar manner when he was implicated as a minor player in the Sharpstown Banking Scandal in the early 1970s, but that was little penance to Galvestonians for what they suffered after his showdown.

The loss of gambling and a padlocked Balinese Room were not the biggest regrets, although even elite businessman I.H. Kempner was concerned that tourists would be incredibly bored without the "Balinese for the well to do and bingo for the medium spender." One thousand people were thrust into the unemployment line after the Free State was shuttered.[313] Hordes of people left the island, and the Galveston economy withered under a summer sun no longer tempered by neon palm trees. One insurance salesman claimed that he lost one hundred policies within sixty days of the raids.[314] Others indirectly victimized were the churches, charities and civic organizations that would no longer benefit from ill-gotten prosperity.[315]

Yet from the beginning, Sam and Rose's ambition was never about gambling, it was about Galveston, and despite how it appeared in the summer of 1957, their legacy was not lost. It took nearly four decades, but Sam and Rose had released the nepotistic vice-grip that, if sustained, would have suffocated the island far more than Wilson's shenanigans. The Free State lives on forever in the hearts of anyone who dares love that tempestuous Texas island as much as the Maceos did. They wanted more for Galveston than profit—they wanted "health for a hundred years."

12

SALUD, CHINDON

Tangibly, not much remains of the Maceos on Galveston Island. The Hollywood Dinner Club tragically burned to the ground during the early morning hours of August 13, 1959. Before it became a warehouse and the setting of the 1957 takedown, it had been unused since the late 1930s, except for hosting a handful of meetings and public dances for the local Jaycees in the mid-1950s. Besides the loss of the historic building, handmade tables and other furniture from the clubs, as well as a collection of life-size German hobby horses from the Racing Derby on the Seawall were stored inside. Galveston's derby carousel was one of only three in the world, and the horses, hand-carved from oak, were considered priceless collector's items. The only evidence left behind from the fire was a cigarette butt on the floor of the foyer, and investigators surmised that it was started by vagrants or vandals.[316] All that remained were the iron gates.

Naturally, rumors circulated that the Maceos burned it down themselves for the insurance money, but they had no reason to burn it down, especially considering its valuable contents.[317] In 1965, the City of Galveston bought the property and the gates as part of the right-of-way acquisition for the Sixty-First Street improvement project that widened the road from two lanes to six. The gates were made freehand and cost more than $2,000 in 1926. They were purchased from the city by Dorris Y. Hutchinson for an underwhelming auction bid of $307.50 and were installed at her Gamboa

An overgrown Hollywood Dinner Club in the late 1950s. *Rosenberg Library.*

Cay property at 7115 Broadway.[318] The gates are still there today, and they are the only publicly viewable remnants from all three of the Maceos' premier nightclubs.

The various clubs and rooms of the Turf Athletic Club building on Market Street were closed along with the Balinese in 1957, and the space was retained by the Maceo family but leased. By the mid-1960s, Maceo and Company could no longer afford to hold its properties. The TAC headquarters were put up for auction and purchased by the First Hutchings and Sealy Bank, which eventually acquired the entire block and razed everything to make room for a modern, style-less monstrosity that sits awkwardly out of place in Galveston's historic downtown. Now, where the Turf Grill served its delicacies and A-list crooners sang the night away at the swanky Studio Lounge, there is only a sidewalk.

At the same 1965 auction, the fabled Balinese Room was also on the block. "We just thought things would be different, that we might be able to get it open again," lamented Sam Serio.[319] Not one person bid on the Balinese Room, but it was finally given new life in 1965 by Johnnie Mitchell, brother of journalist Christie Mitchell. He and Houston oilman John Mecom purchased the famed nightclub for a meager $100,000 and invested another $150,000 in restoring the structure that had been vacant for nearly a decade.[320] Hurricane Carla in 1961 had badly damaged the covered

View of Galveston beach with Balinese Room in background, circa 1980s. *Rosenberg Library*.

The Balinese Room with exterior paint from the 1965 remodel, 1988. *Rosenberg Library*.

Johnny Mitchell rebuilt the foyer off the Seawall into an iconic Asian design that often defines the Balinese Room. *Rosenberg Library.*

walkway, but it was "rebuilt especially for those who believe in the future of the land of sandy beaches, summer homes, happy times, all in this port of paradise, Galveston."[321] The most notable aspect of Mitchell's restoration was the redesign of the front foyer off the Seawall sidewalk. The simple, flat-front 1940s style, with the stretched rectangular awning reminiscent of mid-century condominium buildings in New York City, has been all but forgotten. Mitchell's Asian façade has become so iconic that it is often incorrectly linked to the Maceos.

At first, the new Balinese was a private, members-only club for dinner and dancing (no gambling), but in 1966, it was opened to the public.[322] Mitchell kept the Balinese operating until 1985. Inspired by its renewal, proponents in Galveston tried three times between 1984 and 1988 to pass a non-binding referendum that would be passed along to the state legislature to convince them to create a special casino district on the island. It never made it to Austin, however, and was rejected by the citizens of Galveston all three times. The Balinese Room changed hands several times over the next fifteen years but remained vacant. Time after time, the new owners' plans were never realized.

Aerial view of the Balinese, circa 2000s. *Rosenberg Library.*

Finally, local attorney and entrepreneur Scott Arnold purchased the landmark in 2002 and invested $750,000, converting it into a multivenue with shops, a nightclub and a restaurant. The famous ballroom stayed intact, and Arnold even had the original murals restored.[323] Somehow, something was never quite right about people in blue jeans and T-shirts sitting in metal chairs inside a room that was made famous for its opulence and refinement. Mrs. Rose Maceo, who once turned heads as she arrived in her sequin-studded white gown and floor-length fur coat from Nathan's Department Store, never would have approved. Apparently, neither did Mother Nature. On September 13, 2008, Hurricane Ike did what time could not, and the island was forced to say goodbye to its cherished monument to the good old bad days. For years after Ike, the stunted remains of the wooden pilings peeked out just above the water, as if the island refused to surrender the final vestiges of its beloved Balinese. They were finally extracted in 2013.

The buildings were erased, but the family remained, many of them becoming successful entrepreneurs in their own right. Some of the most high-profile Maceo scions came through the Fertitta line. The Maceo-Fertitta connection goes far beyond the marriage of Sam and Rose's sister Olivia

The Balinese Room after its 2002 purchase by Scott Arnold. *Rosenberg Library*.

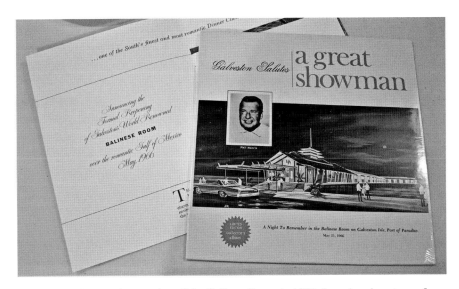

Invitation to the grand reopening of the Balinese Room in 1965, featuring the return of Phil Harris. *Anonymous private collection*.

Hurricane Ike struck the Balinese in 2008, its final undoing. *Rosenberg Library.*

All that remains of Galveston's most famous nightclub is a frame that displays a historical marker commemorating the Balinese Room. *Photo by author.*

Maceo Fertitta to Joseph Frances Fertitta, tracing all the way back to Palermo, Sicily, in the nineteenth century. Joseph's mother was Josephina Serio, sister of Sam and Rose's maternal grandmother, Marianna Serio Sansone, who was the mother of Angelina Sansone Maceo and Concetta Sansone Maceo (matriarchs of the two branches of Maceos in Galveston). Another sister of Angelina and Concetta Sansone Maceo's, Salvatora Sansone, married Joseph Francis Fertitta's brother Salvatore Fertitta. Salvatore and Salvatora Sansone Fertitta were the parents of Guiseppa Fertitta, who married Rosario Charles, Sam and Rose's cousin.[324]

Balinese manager Vic Fertitta's grandson Tilman became a billionaire five times over with the growth and expansion of Landry's Incorporated, which now owns a multitude of pre-established restaurant, hotel and casino chains, such as the Golden Nugget and Galveston's San Luis Resort. Tilman has invested commercially in Galveston, although according to statements he has made to the press, the decision was more about his knowledge of seaside attractions as an ideal investment than any sentimental desire to continue his Maceo family legacy.[325] Unfortunately, the previous misinterpretations and stereotypes that surround the Maceo empire have understandably led to his decision to publicly separate himself from his ancestry, but Tilman's original concepts include a modern incarnation of the Pleasure Pier, constructed in 2012 on the very property where Sam Maceo and W.L. Moody Jr. renovated the municipal pleasure pier in the 1940s, and Vic & Anthony's Steakhouse. On October 6, 2017, the NBA approved Tillman's $1.415 billion purchase of the Houston Rockets, for which he is said to have competed with native Houstonian Beyoncé.

Frank Fertitta Jr. was only four years old when the Balinese room opened, yet he would be the sole member of the Maceo family to forge his way into the casino business from the bottom up, just like his great uncles. His father Frank Sr. had come to Galveston from Leesville with his brothers, Vic and Anthony, and later became a partial owner in Maceo and Company after Sam's death. Senior kept a low profile within the family business, but his son paid close attention to Sam and Rose and seemed naturally inclined to follow in their entertainer footsteps. He moved to Las Vegas at age twenty and started out parking cars, but his charismatic presence soon found a way into low-level management.

He continued to plug away on the strip, spreading his infectious Maceo personality, and soon managed to pull together backing to build an establishment intentionally off the strip in 1976. Ever the innovator like Sam and Rose, Frank Jr. realized that the Vegas locals needed a place to

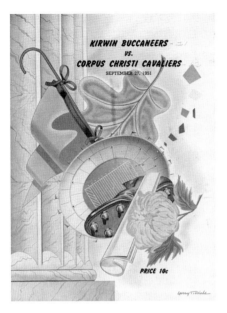

KIRWIN BUCCANEERS
vs.
CORPUS CHRISTI CAVALIERS
SEPTEMBER 27, 1951

PRICE 10c

gamble away from the tourists. He catered to the women and men just getting off work, with cheap 50-cent and dollar tables.[326] First called the Bingo Palace, the name was later changed to Palace Station, and Station Casinos was formed. Station Casinos went public in 1993 and later purchased the Palms Casino Resort for $313 million. Station Casinos owns the Palms, seven Station locations, Red Rock Resort, Graton, Fiesta Henderson and Rancho, four Wildfire locations, Barley's, Lake Mead Lounge and Greens Cafe.

Station Casinos remains the dominant force in the local Vegas market and is currently owned and operated by Frank Jr.'s sons, Frank III and Lorenzo, doubtless named after Lorenzo Grilliette, his great uncle through marriage and longtime Maceo employee. Demonstrating the same genetic resourcefulness as their father and the Maceos, Lorenzo and Frank III purchased a defunct fighting league and transformed it into the worldwide phenomenon known as the Ultimate Fighting Championship (UFC). In 2001, they purchased UFC for $2 million, and that year it tallied 145,000 pay-per-view buys. They changed the format, structured the rules and rebranded the entire business. Within six years, viewership had exploded, and pay-per-views rose to more than 5 million annually. In 2016, Lorenzo and Frank sold 94.2 percent of their stake in UFC for more than $4 billion, then sold the remainder and divested fully the next year. The brothers each have a net worth of nearly $2 billion.[327]

Back in Texas, Vic A. Jr. still owns a seventy-acre Galveston property on the west end that was purchased by his father Gigolo in the late 1950s. After the raids, the bank figured that Gigolo's financial situation was no longer viable and called in his loan. He partnered with his uncles Frank and Vic C. to keep the land, and he raised cattle until his death in 1981.[328]

In Beaumont, Rosario Charles founded TexJoy, purveyor of coffee and spices, with Charlie Fertitta from his wife's side of the family.[329] His daughter Concetta married Jake Tortorice, who purchased, improved and expanded the delectable Rao's Bakery, which was founded in Beaumont

YEA BUCCANEERS, "FIGHT"

Adamcik, Geo. J.
Agruso, Joe
Aiena, Sam
Alarid, Vincent
Albright, Bob
Alessi, G.
Anderson, Henry
Anderson, R. H.
Arenas, John
Astall, Gordon F.
Balducci, Miss Noami
Beaulieu, Clif
Beck, Rev. George A.
Belluomini, E. V.
Biron, A. J.
Boddeker, Louis
Boening, Miss Dorothy
Boening, Miss Mary Beth
Boening, Jr., R. F.
Bogenski, John E.
Bongio, Felix
Branesky, J. W.
Briscoe, D. E.
Brown, LeRoy
Byrne, Wm.
Camano, Rafael
Cannady, John
Cannon, Bob
Cantini, F. O.
Cappadona, Fred J.
Carriere, Ed.
Carter, Sr., A. J.
Carubbi, Angelo J.
Chambers, R. W.
Chataignon, Rt. Rev. Msgr. M. S.
Christensen, Syvert
Chuoke, Robt. C.
Clark, H. W.
Coffey, J. J.
Cordray, Thomas J.
Cox, Rev. John C.
Crawford, Clyde N.
Cuchia, A. J. (Tony)
D'Aloisio, Robert A.
Daly, E. T.
Dantin, R. S.
Depuglio, Vincent
DiBella, Albert J.
DiBella, Frank
DiBella, Joe
Dispensa, Joe
Dispensa, Rosario
Dispensa, Santo
Doherty, A. C.
Donovan, Rev. Thomas A.
Dyball, J. A.
Ecklund, Robert
Eiband, Joe G.
Fabj, Robert
Fertitta, Anthony J.
Fertitta, Mrs. Frank J.
Fertitta, Frank J.
Fertitta, Jr. Frank J.
Fertitta, Joseph S.
Fertitta, Tom A.
Fertitta, Victor J.
Fields, Chick
Fincher, Gaines
Finnegan, Rev. James
Fitzsimmons, George
Fitzsimmons, Mike
Fox, Jr., L. F.

Ganter, Mrs. B. J.
Ganter, B. J.
Garza, Gus
Greaney, George J.
Gremillion, L.
Golden, E. A.
Gonzales, S. P.
Griggs, C. A.
Grilliette, Loranzy
Hannigan, Ray
Harris, STB, Very Rev. Vincent M.
Hartnett, David
Harvey, Emmett
Heath, James L.
Heffernan, Larry
Heins, George
Henderson, William J.
Henry, Morris
Hermann, Julius R.
Hernandez, Sarogoza
Hill, John J.
Holland, Sam
Hopkins, Oscar
Houston, Robert
Hubbell, Bob
Janosky, A. L.
Johnston, Jimmie
Jones, Rev. John B.
Kampe, Heiman
Kearney, Mike
Khaled, Jr., Joe
Kleinecke, H. E.
Kroll, A. J.
Kuhl, Wm. C.
Legge, E. C.
Lera, Jr., Bennie J.
Lera, Thomas A.
Letsos, James
Lewis, Rex
Llewellyn, Earl
Lopez, Sr., Al.
Lopez, Jr., Al.
Lopez, Sr., Joseph
Lopez, Jr., Joseph
Lopez, J. Lewis
Luppens, L. C.
Maceo, Joe T.
Maceo, R. S.
Maceo, Sammie T.
Maceo, Victor A.
Maceo, Victor C.
Maceo, Vincent A.
Macik, Albert
Maechler, Rev. A. M.
Mallia, Allen
Mallia, Eddie
Mallia, Joe L.
Marabella, N.
Marinelli, F. E.
Marinelli, Pete
Martinez, Salvador
Martino, David J.
Matijevch, A.
Matijevich, Steve
Matthews, C. E.
Megna, Joe
Milos, C. D.
Misner, K. H.
Moore, William
Mouton, W. J.
Munivi, Rev. J. T.
McCoy, H. W.

McMaster, William
McNeel, Synott L.
Nicol, Malcom
Nold, STD, Most Rev. W. J.
O'Connell, Rt. Rev. Msgr. D. P.
Ozarchuk, Tony
Paratore, Sr., Phil G.
Paysee, Jack
Perugini, Angelo J.
Perussina, George J.
Perussina, Sam P.
Pistone, Sam
Pistone, Vincent
Porretto, Henry
Pratali, Fred J.
Prino, Jr., Ling B.
Ramirez, Jimmie
Rapp, J. H.
Rapp, R. R.
Rapp, Jr., R. R.
Roach, H. E.
Rogers, Howard
Rourke, Jr., Walter
Rubbright, A. B.
Ruddy, Rev. John J.
Russo Josep F.
Ryder, John
Ryder, J. F.
Sadler, Bill
Sala, Enrico
Salvato, Joe
Sampson, Rev. L. A.
Schoppe, Rev. Charles K.
Schrader, Felix Dutch
Scott, Armie
Serio, Sam
Serio, Vincent S.
Seymour, Raymond F.
Shaw, M. C.
Shepherd, F. J.
Shimek, R. C.
Sitra, Adon
Smith, Wetherill
Strickland, George B.
Stuart, R. A.
Stubbs, T. B.
Sucich, Vido L.
Sudela, Joseph
Sudela, Vincent C.
Sullivan, M. J.
Sunseri, Sr., Frank J.
Sunseri, Jr., Frank J.
Sweeney, J. J.
Tabarracci, Toney
Takacs, Rev. Paul
Tallon, Hugh J.
Termini, D. J.
Thiel, Dr. John M.
Thompson, Jr., H. R.
Tinney, Rev. William L.
Trochesset, Wallace
Uroda, Clement F.
Vaiani, Vaiano
Vallow, Elos J.
Varnell, Joe
Walsh, Edward J.
Waterman, Max
Westrup, William E.
Whelton, Dennis
Williams, Jr., Sam J.
Zapalac, E. F.
Zepeda, Arthur
Zimmerman, R. B.

Opposite: A 1966 football program for Kirwin High School, sponsored by the Maceos. *Author's personal collection.*

Above: The inside of the football program lists Joe T., R.S., Sammie T., Vic A., Vic C. and Vincent Maceo, as well as Sam Serio and Loranzy Grilliette. *Author's personal collection.*

"Slick" and Dorothy Maceo renewing their vows, presided by Father Frank, Maceo family member and beloved parishioner who passed away in 2019. *Family collection.*

and now has four locations throughout Texas. Still in the family, Rao's provides handmade king cakes for purchase at Maceo Spice and Import Company in Galveston during Mardi Gras.

Coincidentally, Galveston's annual Mardi Gras celebration is indirectly attributable to the Maceos, although by way of their unending generosity as opposed to family lineage. Mike Mitchell, formerly Savvas Paraskevopoulos, was a Greek immigrant who settled in Galveston and worked for the Maceo outfit. In the late 1920s, a distraught Mitchell confided in his employers. He said, "I don't know what to do. My son is a genius, but I don't have any money to send him to college." That son was George P. Mitchell, and Sam and Rose Maceo paid for his tuition to Texas A&M University at Galveston.

George Mitchell was the geologist for the Maceo-owned Gulf Oil Properties and went on to perfect the technology of fracking and subsequently acquire a massive fortune through the oil and gas industry. At a chamber of commerce meeting several years before his death in 2013, George Mitchell presented an award to Vic A. Gigolo's son, Vic Jr. "If it weren't for Sam and Rose," Mitchell said proudly, "I never would have gotten to go to Texas A&M."[330] Mitchell invested and donated more than $300 million to Galveston, mostly through the restoration and renovation

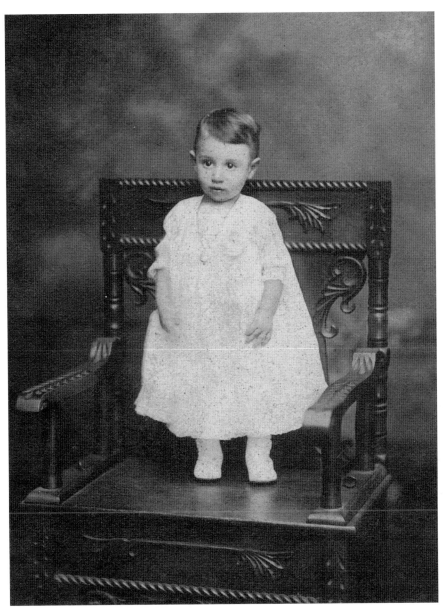

A baby portrait of Slick Maceo. *Family collection.*

of the city's nineteenth century Victorian architecture along the Strand and throughout downtown, incorporating his historic investments under the banner of Mitchell Historic Properties. Mitchell also founded the Wyndham hotel chain, which built the San Luis Resort atop the bunkers of Fort Crockett (later sold to Tilman Fertitta) and currently operates Galveston's only luxury historic hotels, the Hotel Galvez and the Tremont. George Mitchell, along with the nonprofit Galveston Historical Foundation, are given sole credit for rescuing history from the bulldozers and transforming downtown Galveston into a historic destination. As a companion to his architectural efforts, Mitchell revived Mardi Gras on the island in the early 1980s. It was celebrated in Galveston beginning in the 1870s but halted during the Great Depression. Galveston is now home to the third-largest Mardi Gras festival in the United States.

As for the king cakes, they can be found on Market Street inside a nondescript white building—the only one in town to still bear the Maceo name. R.S. "Slick" Maceo founded Maceo Seafood Company in 1944 at the height of the Gulf shrimping boom. Slick was the son of Frank Maceo, the chief investor and head of the Maceo empire after the death of his cousins Sam and Rose. Maceo Seafood Company sold shrimp and other fresh-caught Gulf seafood from a market at Pier 20 in Galveston, but when the shrimping industry plateaued, Slick transitioned by opening Maceo Spice and Import Company. At the time, Slick was unaware that he would be the one to ensure that the Maceo name was never forgotten in Galveston.

That task has now been passed to Slick's son Ronald Maceo and his children. Ronnie's son Frank Maceo is an independent businessman who, in 2016, became one of the youngest members ever elected to the Galveston City Council, and Ronnie's daughter Concetta Maceo works alongside him as a fellow owner and operator of Maceo Spice and Import Company at 2706 Market Street.[331] Following the way of the family, Ronnie has been a restaurateur for decades, owning and operating several different concepts and locations in Austin and Galveston. His daughter Concetta was raised off the island but returned to Galveston in 2014, and what began as part-time help for her father at the shop put her squarely in her element.

Under the leadership of Concetta, unquestionably blessed with the Maceo magic, and in the same space where she stacked boxes into a throne and played "queen of the spices" as a girl, the humble gourmet food store and lunchtime eatery featuring family recipes and house-made spice blends has blossomed into a sought-after island destination and a favorite among

Left: R.S. "Slick" Maceo. *Family collection.*

Below: Maceo Seafood Company's shrimping boat *Ronnie Maceo*. *Family collection.*

Above: R.S. "Slick" Maceo aboard the Maceo Seafood Company vessel *Dorothy Maceo*. *Family collection.*

Opposite, top: Ronald Maceo with his daughter Concetta and son Frank. *Family collection.*

Opposite, bottom: Slick founded Maceo Seafood on the harborside at Pier 20. *Galveston Isle magazine, Rosenberg Library.*

locals. It has also contributed to the formation of the up-and-coming area in Galveston known as West Downtown. In the spirit of her distant cousins Sam and Rose, Concetta carries on a distinct family tradition by hosting free concerts on the store's large side yard. She converted the space into an outdoor music and party venue complete—like the Balinese—with a hand-painted mural by a local artist.

In addition to a long line of successful successors, possibly the greatest Maceo legacy is their story. Penniless Sicilian immigrants rose to fame and fortune amid an island backdrop of a manufactured exclusivity designed to enrich only the few. Instead of succumbing to their surroundings, Sam and Rose played the hand that they were dealt, and in doing so, they not only enriched their family but also all of Galveston. The Maceos transformed Galveston from a serious city of commerce and industry

into a vibrant wellspring of art and culture that defines the community to this day. They not only brought nationwide recognition and world-class entertainment to the city but also revived the unified spirit on which it was built.

Generations after the empire was dismantled, no one on the island speaks ill of the Maceos. Scrutiny and judgment of the alternative economy they established has come only from outsiders looking in on Galveston. Elder locals who lived through the Free State of Galveston remember Sam and Rose with nothing less than fierce admiration and respect. Most importantly, the Maceos singlehandedly changed island culture to reflect their sophisticated philosophies of inclusiveness, generosity, and entrepreneurial inventiveness. The Maceo era is but a memory, but scores of small business owners, artists and philanthropists have continued the diverse and creative commercial tradition set forth by Sam and Rose, working as they did to bring much-deserved acclaim to the island. Now and into the future, the Maceos will be remembered for busting the town wide open.

MACEO FAMILY LINEAGE

For clarity, lineage has been extended only so far as to include the immediate family members of those mentioned or interviewed in the book; it is not intended to represent the entirety of the living Maceo family. Certain married and maiden surnames have been omitted for privacy.

VITO AND ANGELINA MACEO

Vito Maceo (brother of Vincenzo) married Angelina Sansone (sister of Concetta).

They had six children:

1. *Rosario (Rose), married Frances Dispensa. They adopted a son, Rosario Jr.
2. *Salvatore (Sam), married Edna Sedgwick. They had three children, twin boys Salvatore Jr. and Victor Edward (Eddie) and daughter Sedgie.
3. *Vincent C., married Madge. They had one child, Anglia.
4. Thomas Frank (Frank), married his cousin Olivia Maceo (daughter of Vicenzo and Concetta). They had one child, *Vic A. (Gigolo).
   a. *Vic A. married Thelma. They had two children. Vic A. Jr. and Anthony.

5. Olivia, married Joseph Frances Fertitta. They had nine children: *Frank, *Victor, Olivia, *Anthony, Josephine, Sam, Rosario, Joseph and Angelina.

    a. *Frank Fertitta married Johnny "Deady" Grilliette. They had three children, Frank Jr. (father of Frank III and Lorenzo), Joseph and Olivia.

    b. *Victor Fertitta married Mary. They had two children, Olivia and V.J. (father of Tillman, Todd and Jay).

    c. Olivia Fertitta married *Loranzy (Lorenzo) Grilliette.

6. Gaetano, died in Sicily.

VICENZO AND CONCETTA MACEO

Vicenzo Maceo (brother of Vito) married Concetta Sansone (sister of Angelina).

They had seven children:

1. Olivia, married her cousin Thomas Frank (son of Vito and Angelina). They had one child, *Vic A. (Gigolo).

2. *Frank Thomas (Frank), married Katie Lo Piccolo. They had five children: Vincent A., R.S. (Slick), Concetta (Chatta), Florence (Baby) and *Joe T.

    a. *Vincent A. Maceo married Estelle Voight (daughter of *Dutch Voight). They had two children, Vincent Jr. (father of Marlina and Vinny) and Kathryn.

    b. R.S. (Slick) Maceo married Dorothy. They had four children, R.S. Jr., Ronald (father of Concetta and Frank), Olivia and Tommy.

    c. Concetta (Chatta) Maceo married *John Arena. They had three children, Concetta, Mary and David Michael.

    d. Florence married *Bob Fabj.

3. *Vic C., married Katie Gigliotta. They had three children, Vincent G., Annette and Concetta.

4. Rosario Charles, married Giuseppa Fertitta. They had four children, Concetta, Olivia, Sylvina and Theresa.

5. Marianna.

6. Antonino, died in Sicily.

7. *Samuel T. (Little Sammie).

*Denotes family members who worked directly for the Galveston empire.

MACEO SPICE AND IMPORT COMPANY: THE FLAVOR OF AN ISLAND

BY KIMBER FOUNTAIN

This article first appeared in the August 2014 edition of the Island Guide *and is reprinted with their permission.*

The City of Galveston is just over 175 years old, admittedly a rather brief lifespan in the scheme of recorded history, and especially brief when considering that Earth is estimated to have existed for 4.54 billion years. However, during that respectively short amount of time, Galveston and its various residents have witnessed, suffered, endured, thrived, survived, and celebrated enough happenings and happenstance to warrant volumes upon volumes of literary output. The copious number of books written to immortalize Galveston history are collectively representative of the Island's uncanny, chameleonic ability to embrace change without hesitation, and its willingness to adopt a new era of identity as soon as the old one is ushered out. And for each of these eras there has always lingered in the portals of history, a name which unabashedly and courageously defined it. A name that rings with the essence of the Island, a name that conjures images of the fierce and fearless entrepreneurial spirit for which Galveston is known, a name that is a marker for the pride and invincible nature of the Galveston community. Maceo is one of those names.

In a humble little storefront off Market Street, the current generations of Maceos continue their legacy of influence in an equally delightful albeit subtler fashion. Their Spice and Import Company is not only a purveyor of fine foods, fresh, natural spices, and original blends, it is quite literally the cornerstone of Island cuisine. Their seafood seasoning is used in restaurants all over the city, infusing Galveston dining with a distinct flavor, the absence of which is often noticed by locals who are accustomed to the delicious familiarity. Concetta Maceo, whose grandfather R.S. Maceo, Sr. opened the shop in 1944, recalls a new restaurant owner who she assisted. "He was receiving complaints from residents about the way his seafood was seasoned, so I asked him what he was using. When he told me, I told him, 'Well, that was your first mistake,'" she says with a smile, in the trademark, matter of fact, Maceo tone. Then of course she promptly recommended their special blend. "He bought a small amount at first, then called back in a couple of days and ordered a twenty-pound box."

The dynamic impact of their products traces all the way back to the company's roots, as Maceo Spice & Import Company was originally only a wholesale distributor of bulk spices. When Maceo Sr.'s son, Ronald, came into the fold, he injected his remarkable talents as a restaurateur into the business. "My dad knows what people want, he knows what flavors work well together," Concetta says, "and so he started making blends and selling them to restaurants. People would go to the restaurant and say, 'Wow! Where can we get this?' And then they would come to the warehouse and ask how they could purchase it." The demand for Ronald's blends continued to grow, thus prompting him to expand his father's business to include a retail store and eventually, an eatery.

That store has changed locations many times in its seventy years in business; the most memorable one sat at the corner of 25th and Market. "At that time, this was just a packing house," Ronald's daughter remembers. "But after Hurricane Ike took that store, my Dad decided to combine it all into this building." The Spice Company sells all of their spices in both individual and wholesale amounts and will also craft special custom blends for a restaurant. Sometimes they will take a restaurant's pre-existing recipe blend and recreate it in bulk. "Of course, we keep all of the recipes confidential," Concetta explains, "but having us make your spices in bulk for you really increases the consistency and efficiency of commercial kitchens." All of their spices are MSG-free, with no additives or anti-caking agents. "It's just a pure, quality product," she continues, and names their specialty as the salt-free blends they offer. Salt intake is a hot-button issue among nutritionists and health-conscious eaters, so the specialty blends allow for a full, savory seasoning without the need for salt.

The "Import" side of Maceo's Spice & Import Company includes a delectable selection of many exotic and finer foods including olive oil imported from Italy, Red and Black Caviar, gourmet cheeses and meats, and other rare, hard to find international cooking essentials. Products from nearly every continent line the shelves, as well as regionally and locally small batch produced items. Pastas, rice, vinegars, oils, and canned delicacies represent a world tour of luxurious eating.

Lunch at Maceo's is too an authentic and flavorful affair, with specialty Italian sandwiches like the Sopressata, an Italian salami with provolone, or the Caprese, with layers of basil, fresh tomatoes, and whole mozzarella. "If I could only say one thing, though, it would be 'get the Muffaletta.'" Concetta affirms it is undoubtedly the best, made in the authentic New Orleans style on Italian loaf bread with ham, salami, provolone, and Maceo's Olive Salad. Then she adds, "And the Tomato Gravy, and our dipping spices." The dipping spices are available in individual quantities, or for just a little more than the price of a bag, they will serve it up with a loaf of homemade bread and olive oil. In addition to their regularly offered menu there are also daily specials, most often dependent on whatever Ronald feels like making that day. They have recently, however, in the vein of traditional New Orleans restaurants, added the regular Monday special of Pork Chops with Red Beans & Rice.

For a while, Maceo's had significantly reduced their lunch offerings, but fortunately for their loyal following the spice shop is again the perfect out-of-the-way spot for a quiet lunch or an afternoon with close friends. "I just want this to be a place where people can relax, and just enjoy the atmosphere," Concetta Maceo says, "This is a great place." Indeed, the juxtaposition of generations on this small little spice shop is undeniable. Just as Ronald pushed the envelope with his father all those years ago, Concetta is once again reimagining the store to appeal to current generations. She has applied for a liquor license, so they will soon be serving beer and wine, and will add imported wines to their inventory. Her ultimate goal is to complete her studies at UTMB and become a Nurse Practitioner, but in the meantime, Concetta Maceo keeps the torch burning, and adds her own zest to a family name that has never failed to spice up Island life.

MACEO SPICE & IMPORT COMPANY
2706 Market St.
409.763.3331
www.MaceoSpice.com
Tuesday–Saturday, 11:00 a.m.–5:00 p.m.
Sunday, 10:00 a.m.–2:00 p.m.

NOTES

Chapter 1

1. Raab, *Five Families*, 13.
2. Smith, *Complete History*, 15.
3. Raab, *Five Families*, 14.
4. Smith, *Complete History*, 19.
5. Davis, *Mafia Kingfish*, 23–24.
6. Lunde, *Organized Crime*, 55–56.
7. Ibid., 56.
8. Davis, *Mafia Kingfish*, 25.
9. Lunde, *Organized Crime*, 57.
10. Davis, *Mafia Kingfish*, 23–24.
11. Raab, *Five Families*, 15.
12. Lunde, *Organized Crime*, 57.
13. Ibid.
14. Raab, *Five Families*, 16–17.
15. Lunde, *Organized Crime*, 57.
16. Raab, *Five Families*, 19–20.
17. Ibid., 20.
18. Ibid., 13.
19. Lunde, *Organized Crime*, 56.
20. Lineage compiled by author via family interviews, various references and Ancestry.com.
21. Ibid.

22. Pictured, accessed via Ancestry.com
23. Family correspondence.

Chapter 2

24. Davis, *Mafia Kingfish*, 19.
25. Ibid., 27, 22.
26. Ibid., 27–29.
27. Vic A. Maceo interview by author.
28. Ancestry.com family tree compiled by author.
29. List or Manifest of Alien Passengers, April 21, 1904.
30. Thirteenth Census of the United States, ancestry.com.
31. Ancestry.com family tree.
32. Fourteenth Census of the United States, ancestry.com.
33. *1911–1912 General Directory*.
34. *1913 General Directory*.
35. WWI Draft Registration, Salvatore Maceo, ancestry.com.
36. U.S. Department of Labor Petition, Salvatore Maceo.
37. WWI Draft Registration, Rosario Maceo, ancestry.com.
38. *1911–1912 General Directory*.
39. "Maceo and Torregrosso," *Galveston Daily News*.
40. "Body Found," *Galveston Daily News*; "Reward Is Offered," *Galveston Daily News*; "Arrest Still Lacking," *Galveston Daily News*.
41. Vic A. Maceo interview.
42. Saralyn Richardson interview.

Chapter 3

43. Greene, "More Than a Thimbleful," 46.
44. Waldman, "Casinos."
45. Nieman, "Galveston's Balinese Room."
46. Chalfant, *Galveston Island of Chance*, 86.
47. Waldman, "Casinos."
48. Cartwright, *Galveston*, 209.
49. Ibid.
50. Waldman, "Casinos."
51. Waldman, "Bootleggers."

52. Ibid.
53. Ibid.
54. Thornton, "Policy Analysis No. 157."
55. Greene, "More Than a Thimbleful," 46.
56. Thornton, "Cato Institute Policy."
57. Ibid.
58. Greene, "More Than a Thimbleful," 46.
59. Waldman, "Bootleggers."
60. Scarlett, "Back to the Balinese."
61. Cartwright, *Galveston*, 213.

Chapter 4

62. Cartwright, *Galveston*, 212.
63. Waldman, "Bootleggers."
64. Greene, "More Than a Thimbleful."
65. Scarlett, "Back to the Balinese."
66. Waldman, "Bootleggers."
67. Vic Maceo interview.
68. Waldman, "Bootleggers."
69. Mitchell, "Beachcomber," January 20, 1974.
70. Greene, "More Than a Thimbleful."
71. Ibid.
72. "Government Denies," *Galveston Daily News*.
73. Vic Maceo interview.
74. Scarlett, "Back to the Balinese"; "Agents Nab Head," *Galveston Daily News*.
75. Waldman, "Bootleggers."
76. Ibid.
77. Vic Maceo interview.
78. Waldman, "Bootleggers."
79. Greene, "More Than a Thimbleful."
80. Waldman, "Bootleggers."
81. Greene, "More Than a Thimbleful."
82. Ibid.
83. Waldman, "Bootleggers."
84. "Mash" is crushed malt or grain that is steeped in boiling water to create wort, a sweet liquid that is siphoned off the mash and then fermented to make beer or whiskey.

85. Greene, "More Than a Thimbleful."
86. Ibid.
87. Ibid.

Chapter 5

88. Lauersdorf, "Galveston's Balinese Room."
89. "Bathing Girl Revue, To Be Riot," *Galveston Daily News*.
90. "Draws Great Crowds," *Galveston Daily News*.
91. "C. of C. Goal," *Galveston Daily News*.
92. "New Amusement Places," *Galveston Daily News*.
93. "Playground of Southwest," *Galveston Daily News*.
94. "Two Galvestonians," *Galveston Daily News*.
95. Waldman, "Bootleggers."
96. "Rosalie M. Case," *Galveston Daily News*.
97. "Five Defendants," *Galveston Daily News*.
98. "Nounes-Varnell," *Galveston Daily News*.
99. Waldman, "Bootleggers."
100. Swanson, *Blood Aces*, 231.
101. Vic Maceo interview.
102. Cartwright, *Galveston*, 213.
103. "Will Move Radio Station to Club," *Galveston Daily News*.
104. "Hollywood Club," *Galveston Daily News*.
105. "Local Entertainer," *Galveston Daily News*.
106. "Brilliant Night," *Galveston Daily News*.
107. "Postpone Opening," *Galveston Daily News*.
108. "Auspicious Opening," *Galveston Daily News*.
109. "Hollywood to Reopen for Season," *Galveston Daily News*.
110. "Club to Close," *Galveston Daily News*; "Club Faces Contempt," *Galveston Daily News*.
111. "Club Injunctions," *Galveston Daily News*.
112. Court proceedings, *Galveston Daily News*, November 7, 1929.
113. Waldman, "Bootleggers."
114. Ibid.
115. Ibid.
116. Lait and Mortimer, *U.S.A. Confidential*, 216.

Chapter 6

117. "Shooting of Maledo," *Galveston Daily News*.

118. "Charges are Dismissed," *Galveston Daily News*.

119. "Quinn's Body Here," *Galveston Daily News*.

120. "Nounes and Musey in Jail," *Galveston Daily News*.

121. "Nounes and Musey Get Prison," *Galveston Daily News*.

122. "Musey Is Indicted," *Galveston Daily News*.

123. "Nounes and Etie," *Corsicana Daily Sun*.

124. "Alleged Rum Runners," *Galveston Tribune*; "Houston Rum Runner Sentenced," *Corsicana Daily Sun*.

125. "Musey's $10,000 Bond," *Galveston Tribune*.

126. *Galveston Daily News*, August 13–14, 1931.

127. Cartwright, *Galveston*, 215.

128. Franks, "Maceos."

129. Estate of Maceo vs. Commissioner.

130. "Sui Jen, Galveston's Newest," *Galveston Daily News*; "Sui Jen Against Swee," *Galveston Daily News*.

131. "Swee Ren vs. Sui Jen," *Galveston Daily News*.

132. "Book by Learned Orientalist," *Galveston Daily News*.

133. "Eagle Praises Galveston," *Galveston Daily News*.

134. Ibid.

135. Ibid.

136. Greene, "More Than a Thimbleful."

137. "Island Liquor Gangs," *Galveston Daily News*.

138. "Liquor Indictment," *Galveston Daily News*.

139. "Dutch Voight Pays Fine," *Galveston Tribune*.

140. Marlina Maceo interview.

141. "Nounes Likes to See," *Galveston Daily News*.

142. "Brothers on Trial," *Corsicana Daily Sun*.

143. "Pair Fined on Assault," *Galveston Daily News*.

144. "Nounes Fined," *Galveston Daily News*.

145. "Nounes is Charged in Holdup," *Valley Morning Star*.

146. "Liquor Charges are Filed Here," *Galveston Tribune*; "Sought in Liquor Case," *Port Arthur News*; "Liquor Trials," *Galveston Daily News*.

147. "Nine Named in Vote Frauds Make Bonds," *Galveston Daily News*; "Nounes Guilty in Vote Case," *Galveston Daily News*.

148. "Case Against Barge Owner," *Galveston Daily News*.

149. "Contempt in Musey Case," *Galveston Daily News*.

150. "Gaming Cases Set for Today," *Galveston Daily News*; "Pool Hall Cases Dismissed Here," *Galveston Daily News*.
151. "Hearing for Goss," *Galveston Daily News*.
152. Ibid.
153. Ibid.
154. Ibid.
155. Ronald Maceo interview.
156. Nieman, "Galveston's Balinese Room."

Chapter 7

157. Swanson, *Blood Aces*, 52.
158. Lait and Mortimer, *U.S.A. Confidential*, 216.
159. Pittman and Eaves, "Main Figures: Carlos Marcello."
160. Waldman, "Big Sam and Papa Rose."
161. Waldman, "Bootleggers."
162. Vic Maceo interview.
163. Waldman, "Big Sam and Papa Rose."
164. Vic Maceo interview.
165. Davis, *Mafia Kingfish*, 38–43.
166. Pittman and Eaves, "Main Figures: Carlos Marcello."
167. Finstuen, "Fred Musey."
168. Cabot, "Marijuana—Weed of Sin."
169. Ibid.; *Galveston Daily News*, "George Musey."
170. Davis, *Mafia Kingfish*, 40.
171. *Galveston Daily News*, "Hearing for Goss."
172. Ronald Maceo interview.
173. Lait and Mortimer, *U.S.A. Confidential*, 218.
174. Ronald Maceo interview.
175. Swanson, *Blood Aces*, 52.
176. Ibid., 53.
177. Denton and Morris, *Money and the Power*, 31.
178. Swanson, *Blood Aces*, 56.
179. "George Musey," *Galveston Daily News*.
180. "Narcotic Case," *Galveston Daily News*.
181. "Jury Unable to Agree," *Galveston Tribune*.
182. "Maceo Acquitted," *Galveston Daily News*.
183. Waldman, "Big Sam and Papa Rose."

184. "Jury Unable to Agree," *Galveston Tribune*.
185. "Narcotic Case," *Galveston Daily News*.
186. Kelso, "Aces High."
187. Lomax, "Murder of Vincent Vallone."
188. Ibid.
189. Ibid.
190. Ibid.
191. Ibid.
192. Davis, *Mafia Kingfish*, 71.
193. Vic Maceo interview.
194. Denton and Morris, *Money and the Power*, 55.
195. Vic Maceo interview.

Chapter 8

196. Ronald Maceo interview.
197. Chalfant, *Galveston Island of Chance*, 150.
198. Waldman, "Casinos."
199. Chalfant, *Galveston Island of Chance*, 31.
200. Ibid.
201. Ibid.
202. Estate of Maceo vs. Commissioner.
203. Waldman, "Gamblers."
204. Ibid.
205. Ibid.
206. "Beach Bathhouse Is Purchased," *Galveston Daily News*.
207. Vic Maceo interview.
208. Often misspelled as *Quadri*.
209. Dinibeth, "Mary Go Round."
210. Maceo, "Remembering the Balinese Room."
211. Mitchell, *Night Owl*, 227.
212. Lauersdorf, "Galveston's Balinese Room."
213. "L-Men Seize Half Case," *Galveston Tribune*.
214. Waldman, "Casinos."
215. Vic Maceo interview.
216. Frank Maceo interview.
217. "As We Saw It," *Austin American Statesman*.
218. Waldman, "Gamblers."

219. Franks, "Maceos."
220. Ibid.
221. Waldman, "Casinos."
222. "Ornate Gates Purchased," *Galveston Daily News*.
223. Cherry, "Galveston Gambling Dynasty."
224. Waldman, "Casinos."
225. "Who's Who," *Galveston Isle*.
226. Waldman, "Casinos."
227. Mitchell, *Night Owl*, 136–38.
228. "Phil and Alice," *Galveston Daily News*.
229. Waldman, "Casinos."
230. Vic Maceo interview.
231. Ibid.

Chapter 9

232. Lait and Mortimer, *U.S.A. Confidential*, 214.
233. Cherry, "Galveston's Gambling Dynasty."
234. Vic Maceo interview.
235. Cherry, "Galveston's Gambling Dynasty."
236. Mitchell, *Night Owl*, 72.
237. Waldman, "Big Sam and Papa Rose."
238. Mitchell, "Opening with a Splash."
239. Chalfant, *Galveston Island of Chance*, 20–21.
240. Ibid., 20–21, 32.
241. Cherry, "Galveston's Gambling Dynasty."
242. Waldman, "Big Sam and Papa Rose."
243. Ronald Maceo interview.
244. Mitchell, *Night Owl*, 115.
245. Waldman, "Big Sam and Papa Rose."
246. Lait and Mortimer, *U.S.A. Confidential*, 216.
247. Ibid.
248. Vic Maceo interview.
249. Ronald Maceo interview.
250. Mitchell, *Night Owl*, 23; Waldman, "Gamblers."
251. "Who's Who," *Galveston Isle*.
252. Mitchell, "Yours for Fun."
253. Waldman, "Big Sam and Papa Rose."

Chapter 10

254. Mitchell, *Night Owl*, 65.
255. Hammer, *Playboy's Illustrated History*, 218.
256. Ibid., 220.
257. Ibid., 222–23.
258. Ibid., 224.
259. Rothman, *Neon Metropolis*, 13.
260. Denton and Morris, *Money and the Power*, 46–47.
261. Vic Maceo interview.
262. Newton, *Mr. Mob*, 137.
263. Denton and Morris, *Money and the Power*, 47.
264. Newton, *Mr. Mob*, 138.
265. Vic Maceo interview.
266. Hammer, *Playboy's Illustrated History*, 224.
267. Franks, "Maceos."
268. Mitchell, *Night Owl*, 138.
269. Vic Maceo interview.
270. "Sam Maceo Dies," *Galveston Daily News*.
271. Lait and Mortimer, *U.S.A. Confidential*, 215.
272. Ronald Maceo interview.
273. Vic Maceo interview.
274. Waldron, "Intrigue, Texas Size."
275. Ibid.
276. Ibid.

Chapter 11

277. "State Crime Hunters," *Galveston Daily News*.
278. Goodenow, "Maceo Men Won't Talk."
279. Vic Maceo interview.
280. Waldman, "Decline and Fall."
281. Long, "Shutdown."
282. Waldman, "Decline and Fall."
283. Estate of Maceo vs. Commissioner.
284. Ronald Maceo interview.
285. Cabot, "Marijuana—Weed of Sin."
286. Mitchell, "The Beachcomber."

287. Ely, "Fabled B-Room."
288. Letter from D.W. Kempner to Mary Jean, May 19, 1956.
289. Ronald Maceo interview.
290. Suydam, "Wide-Open Galveston."
291. Skelton, "Galveston 'Clean, Open.'"
292. Galveston Chamber of Commerce, September 23, 1955.
293. Clough, "Why I Want Galveston."
294. "Galveston: Wide-Open Sin Town," *Tempo*.
295. "Maceo Figures in Tax Evasion Case," *Galveston Daily News*.
296. Waldman, "Decline and Fall."
297. Nieman, "Galveston's Balinese Room."
298. "Prostitution in Galveston," American Social Health Association Records, folder 110:8.
299. Suydam, "Wide-Open Galveston."
300. Ibid.
301. Nieman, "Galveston's Balinese Room."
302. Ibid.
303. Ronald Maceo interview.
304. Nieman, "Galveston's Balinese Room."
305. Long, "Shutdown."
306. Nieman, "Galveston's Balinese Room."
307. "As We Saw It," *Austin American Statesman*.
308. Long, "Shutdown."
309. Nieman, "Galveston's Balinese Room."
310. Ibid.
311. Script from WBAP-TV/NBC, June 21, 1957.
312. "Prostitution in Galveston," American Social Health Association Records, folder 110:8.
313. Letter from I.H. to Cecile Kempner, June 18, 1951.
314. Waldman, "Decline and Fall."
315. Letter from I.H. to Cecile Kempner, June 18, 1951.

Chapter 12

316. "Smoldering Club, Embers Wetted," *Galveston Tribune*.
317. Vic Maceo interview.
318. "Ornate Gates Purchased," *Galveston Daily News*.
319. Ely, "B Room on Block."

320. Barrileaux, "B-Room Goes Public."
321. Member Letter from Johnny Mitchell, March 1971.
322. Barrileaux, "B-Room Goes Public."
323. Streuli, "Houston Investor Gambles."
324. Ancestry.com.
325. Melby, "The World's Richest Restaurateur."
326. Vic and Ronald Maceo interview.
327. Miller, "Ultimate Cash Machine."
328. Vic Maceo interview.
329. Ronald Maceo interview.
330. Vic Maceo interview.
331. See Appendix B.

BIBLIOGRAPHY

Books

1911–1912 General Directory of the City of Galveston. Galveston, TX: Morrison and Fourmy Directory Company, 1911.

1913 General Directory of the City of Galveston. Galveston, TX: Morrison and Fourmy Directory Company, 1913.

Cartwright, Gary. *Galveston: A History of the Island.* New York: MacMillan, 1991.

Chalfant, Frank E. *Galveston Island of Chance.* Houston: Treasures of Nostalgia, 1997.

Davis, John H. *Mafia Kingfish: Carlos Marcello and the Assassination of John F. Kennedy.* New York: McGraw-Hill, 1989.

Denton, Sally, and Roger Morris. *The Money and the Power: The Making of Las Vegas and Its Hold on America, 1947–2000.* New York: Knopf and Borzoi (Random House), 2001.

Hammer, Richard. *Playboy's Illustrated History of Organized Crime.* Chicago: Playboy, 1975.

Lait, Jack, and Lee Mortimer. *U.S.A. Confidential: The Low-Down on All of Us.* New York: Crown, 1952.

Lunde, Paul. *Organized Crime: An Inside Guide to the World's Most Successful Industry.* London: Dorling Kindersley, 2004.

Mitchell, Christie. *The Night Owl: Reminiscences of Galveston's Famous Night Life.* Complied by Bill Cherry. Self-published, CreateSpace, 2011.

Newton, Michael. *Mr. Mob: The Life and Crimes of Moe Dalitz*. Jefferson, NC: McFarland, 2007.

Raab, Selwyn. *Five Families: The Rise, Decline, and Resurgence of America's Most Powerful Mafia Empires*. New York: St. Martin's, 2005.

Rothman, Hal. *Neon Metropolis: How Las Vegas Started the Twenty-First Century*. New York: Routledge, 2002.

Smith, Jo Durden. *A Complete History of the Mafia*. New York: MetroBooks, 2005.

Swanson, Doug J. *Blood Aces: The Wild Ride of Benny Binion, the Texas Gangster Who Created Vegas Poker*. New York: Penguin, 2014.

Articles

Austin American Statesman. "As We Saw It: High-Stakes Entertainment." March 2, 1986.

Barrileaux, Gladys. "B-Room Goes Public Friday." *Galveston Daily News*, September 5, 1967.

Brigane, Jim, and Dan McDonald. "The Mob Is Moving into Texas." *San Antonio Express*, January 11, 1976.

Cabot, Heloise. "Marijuana—Weed of Sin." *American Detective*, August 1938.

Cartwright, Gary. "Benny and the Boys." *Texas Monthly*, September 30, 1991.

———. "One Last Shot." *Texas Monthly*, June 1993.

Cherry, Bill. "Galveston's Gambling Dynasty: The Maceo Family." *Texas Heritage*, 2011.

Clough, Roy. As told to Michael Dorman. "Why I Want Galveston an Open Town!" *Man's Magazine*, October 1955.

Corsicana Sun. "Brothers on Trial for Intimidation Federal Witnesses." March 10, 1931.

———. "Galveston Rum Ring Sent to Prison for Two Years Each." May 18, 1929.

———. "Houston Rum Runner Sentenced on Tuesday." February 25, 1930.

———. "Nounes and Etie Given Instructed Acquittal Verdict." October 30, 1929.

Dinibeth. "Mary Go Round." Society Column. *Galveston Daily News*, January 23, 1942.

Ely, Jane. "Fabled B Room on Block." *Houston Post*, May 27, 1965.

Finstuen, Doc. "Fred Musey: Galveston Bootlegger and Club Operator." *Lookout Journal* 1, no. 1 (January 2002).

Franks, Zarko. "The Maceos: Isle's 'Good Old Bad Days' Remembered." *Houston Chronicle*, July 24, 1977.

Galveston Daily News. "Argument and Threats Preceded Shooting of Maledo, Witness Says." March 1, 1928.

———. "Arrest Still Lacking in Maceo Murder Mystery." November 16, 1921.

———. "Bathing Girl Revue Draws Great Crowds." May 24, 1920.

———. "Bathing Girl Revue, To Be Riot of Color and Style, Will Be Held on Beach Today." May 23, 1920.

———. "Betty Pat Trial Set for Hearing Today." March 28, 1925.

———. "Body Found with Head Crushed In." November 4, 1921.

———. "Book by Learned Orientalist Gave Name to Sui Jen." December 14, 1932.

———. "Both Sides Ready in Rosalie M. Case." March 31, 1925.

———. "Case Against Barge Owner Is Continued." May 27, 1954.

———. "Club to Close Tomorrow Night." August 19, 1927.

———. "C. of C. Goal Is Set at 2,000 Members; Dinner for New Men Is Declared 'One of Best Ever Held.'" August 30, 1924.

———. "Conflicts in Testimony of Gin Witnesses." May 9, 1929.

———. "The Courts." November 7, 1929.

———. "Death Blow to Rum Traffic Seen; Customs Men Jubilant as Alleged Gang Leaders Held." August 14, 1931.

———. "Eagle Praises Galveston in Address for Its Refusal to 'Surrender' to Liquor Law." August 25, 1933.

———. "Etie Case Going to Jurors Today." March 11, 1931.

———. "Five Defendants in Liquor Case Freed." April 10, 1925.

———. "Former Coast Guard Officer Arrested; Musey Is Indicted." January 28, 1930.

———. "George Musey Says He's Broke but Glad to Be Back." August 14, 1931.

———. "Government Denies Having Agreement with George Musey." August 20, 1931.

———. "Hearing Set on Club Injunctions; State Determined to Put Stop to Gambling." July 3, 1928.

———. "Hollywood Club to Open May 11." May 4, 1927.

———. "Hollywood Club to Reopen for Season." May 11, 1927.

———. "Hollywood Club to Use English Ideas." June 30, 1926.

———. "Hollywood Plans a Brilliant Night." September 1, 1926.

———. "Hollywood Winter Season Has an Auspicious Opening." November 17, 1926.

―――. "Island Is Called Playground of Southwest." May 13, 1925.

―――. "Island's Liquor Gangs Are Objects of Attack by Prohibition Forces." February 14, 1932.

―――. "Johnny Jack Is Fined Again on Sale of Liquor." February 26, 1936.

―――. "Liquor Trials." October 10, 1943.

―――. "Local Entertainer Is Chicago Success." October 21, 1926.

―――. "Maceo and Torregrosso." December 18, 1918.

―――. "Musey Attorneys Have Short Time Left for Appeal." February 15, 1930.

―――. "New Amusement Places Popular; Effort Made to Provide High-Class Eating Resorts Here." January 5, 1925.

―――. "Night Club Faces Contempt Citation." August 19, 1927.

―――. "Nine Named in Vote Frauds Make Bonds." September 21, 1948.

―――. "Nounes and Musey Get Prison Term." May 19, 1929.

―――. "Nounes and Musey in Jail Her to Await Sentence of Court." May 12, 1929.

―――. "Nounes Fined $500 on Liquor Charges." February 13, 1936.

―――. "Nounes Guilty in Vote Case." October 12, 1949.

―――. "Nounes Likes to See His Name in Print." July 13, 1930.

―――. "Nounes-Varnell to Be Given Sentences; Supreme Court Mandate Is Returned; Convicted on Liquor Counts." June 16, 1925.

―――. "Ollie Quinn: Charges Are Dismissed." April 19, 1929.

―――. "Ornate Gates Purchased." September 24, 1965.

―――. "Pair Fined on Assault Charges." October 17, 1933.

―――. "Postpone Opening of Hollywood Club." October 17, 1926.

―――. "Quinn's Body Here After Fatal Crash." August 24, 1949.

―――. "Quinn Trial in Gambling Case Today." October 17, 1929.

―――. "Reward Is Offered in Maceo Mystery." November 6, 1921.

―――. "Rum War Arrests Make Bond." February 28, 1924.

―――. "Sam Maceo Dies in Baltimore Hospital." April 17, 1951.

―――. "State Crime Hunters Set Galveston Probe; Rose Maceo, 5 Aides Go to Austin Today." June 1, 1951.

―――. "Sui Jen Against Swee Ren Latest Topic of Debate." December 11, 1932.

―――. "Sui Jen, Galveston's Newest Night Rendezvous, Ready for Gala Opening Scene Tonight." November 2, 1932.

―――. "Swee Ren vs. Sui Jen." December 11, 1932.

―――. "Two Galvestonians and Crew of British Schooner Face Charges." January 9, 1924.

———. "U.S. Agents Nab Head of Local Gang in Louisiana; Search Led Police into Many Lands; Agents Refuse to Divulge Details." August 13, 1931.

———. "Varnell-Nounes Appeal Expected to Come up at New Orleans Next Month." January 10, 1925.

———. "Will Move Radio Station to Club." June 4, 1926.

Galveston Isle. "A Good Samaritan Has Passed On." May 1951.

———. "Phil and Alice Arrive in City Today; Marriage Set Next Week." September 13, 1941.

———. "Who's Who." January–February 1948.

Galveston Tribune. "Alleged Rum Runners Given 2-Year Terms." January 29, 1930.

———. "Capt. Le Duc Fined for Contempt in Musey Case." June 23, 1928.

———. "'Dutch' Voight Pays Fine for Smuggling Rum." January 20, 1934.

———. "Gaming Cases Set for Today." October 24, 1928.

———. "Johnny Jack Faces New Liquor Charges." September 27, 1934.

———. "Jury Unable to Agree in Maceo Case; Schipano Convicted; Jurors to Resume Deliberations This Morning." October 24, 1942.

———. "Liquor Charges are Filed Here." March 10, 1943.

———. "L-Men Seize Half Case of Liquor in 3-Hour Search of Balinese Room; Charges to be Filed, Supervisor Says. March 6, 1943.

———. "Maceo Acquitted in New York Narcotics Trial." October 25, 1942.

———. "Men Make Bond on Liquor Indictment." March 7, 1933.

———. "Musey's $10,000 Bond Largest to Be Forfeited." April 11, 1930.

———. "Pool Hall Cases Dismissed Here." November 24, 1928.

———. "Smoldering Club, Embers Wetted." August 13, 1959.

Goodenow, Laura. "Maceo Men Won't Talk: Quiz to Enter New Phase." *Galveston Daily News*, June 26, 1951.

Greene, Casey Edward. "More Than a Thimbleful: Prohibition in Galveston, 1919–1933." *Houston Review* 6 (1989), 45–56.

Heller, Mike. "Galveston: Open City of Sin." *Eye*. January 1957.

Huckaby, Sarah. "In Nightlife Heyday Burned Club Was Gulf Gaming Mecca." *Galveston Daily News*, August 13, 1959.

Kelso, Jennifer. "Aces High: The Maceo Legend." *Texas Historian* 46, no. 2 (November 1985).

Lauersdorf, Cheryl. "Galveston's Balinese Room Presents Bootleggers, Big Bands, High Rollers, and Headliners." *Touchstone*, 2013.

Lomax, John Nova. "The Murder of Vincent Vallone." *Texas Monthly*, June 30, 2016.

Long, Steven. "Shutdown: June 10, 1957, the Day the Wheels Stopped Turning." *In Between*, December 1983.

Maceo, Peggy. "Remembering the Balinese Room." *Texas Monthly*, January 20, 2013.

Melby, Caleb. "The World's Richest Restaurateur Has a Secret: It's Not About the Food." *Forbes*, August 23, 2012.

Miller, Matthew G. "Blood Brothers: Frank and Lorenzo Fertitta." *Bloomberg Markets*, September 2012.

———. "Ultimate Cash Machine." *Forbes*, May 5, 2008.

Mitchell, Christie. "The Beachcomber." *Galveston Daily News*, October 17, 1954.

———. "Opening with a Splash." *Galveston Isle*, May 1948.

———. "Yours for Fun." *Galveston Isle*, January–February 1948.

Nieman, Robert. "Galveston's Balinese Room." *Texas Ranger Dispatch*, July 2017.

Pittman, Mark, and Richard Eaves. "Main Figures: Carlos Marcello." *Girl Who Shot JFK* (blog). https://www.thegirlwhoshotjfk.com.

Port Arthur News. "Brazoria Sheriff Confers Here on Robbery Case." January 14, 1940.

———. "Hearing for Johnny Jack Today." January 18, 1940.

———. "Last of Liquor Ring to Be Tried; Five of Men Already Have Been Sentenced." March 16, 1930.

———. "Receives Third Fine." April 8, 1936.

———. "Sought in Liquor Case." August 12, 1943.

Scarlett, Harold. "Back to the Balinese." *Houston Post*, December 16, 1990.

Skelton, Max B. "Galveston 'Clean, Open' New Mayor." *Rome Daily American*, May 25, 1955.

Streuli, Ted. "Houston Investor Gambles on a Multivenue at Balinese Room." *Galveston Daily News*, April 22, 2002.

Suydam, Henry. "Wide-Open Galveston Mocks Texas Laws." *Life*, August 15, 1955.

Valley Morning Star. "Nounes Is Charged in Holdup." January 12, 1940.

Waldman, Alan. "Isle of Illicit Pleasures: Part I: The Bootleggers." *In Between*, March 1979.

———. "Isle of Illicit Pleasures: Part II: Prostitution." *In Between*, April 1979.

———. "Isle of Illicit Pleasures: Part III: The Casinos." *In Between*, May 1979.

———. "Isle of Illicit Pleasures: Part IV: The Gamblers." *In Between*, June 1979.

————. "Isle of Illicit Pleasures: Part V: Big Sam and Papa Rose." *In Between*, July 1979.

————. "Isle of Illicit Pleasures: Part VI: The Decline and Fall." *In Between*, August 1979.

Waldron, Martin. "Intrigue, Texas Size." *New York Times*, February 6, 1972.

Webb, Joe. "Narcotic Case Bonds Total $135,000; Sam Maceo Is Charged Here as 16 Nabbed." *Galveston Daily News*, October 6, 1937.

Theses

Brown, Jean M. "Free Rein: Galveston Island's Alcohol, Gambling, and Prostitution Era, 1839–1957." Master's thesis, College of Graduate Studies at Lamar University, August 1998.

Reports

Hotel Galvez. National Register of Historic Places Inventory—Nomination Form #79002944. April 4, 1979.

"Proceedings of September 23, 1955." Galveston Chamber of Commerce Records.

"Prostitution in Galveston, Texas." Documents from 1949–60 selected from boxes 109–110 in the American Social Health Association Records. Social Welfare History Archives. University of Minnesota Libraries, 1992.

Thornton, Mark. "Cato Institute Policy Analysis No. 157: Alcohol Prohibition Was a Failure." July 17, 1991.

Interviews and Personal Correspondences

Family email correspondence regarding the immigration of Vicenzo and Concetta Maceo. March 5, 2010.

Frank Maceo interview by author. April 3, 2019.

Marlina Maceo interview by author. April 10, 2019.

Ronald Maceo interview by author. April 3, 2019.

Saralyn Richardson interview by author. May 9, 2019.

Vic A. Maceo Jr. interview by author. April 3, 2019 and June 23, 2019.

Miscellaneous

Estate of Maceo v. Commissioner, 23 T.C.M. 258 (U.S. Tax 1964).

Fourteenth Census of the United States: 1920—Population. Orleans County, New Orleans. Ancestry.com.

Letter from D.W. Kempner to Mary Jean. May 19, 1956. Harris and Eliza Kempner Collection. Rosenberg Library.

Letter from I.H. Kempner to Cecile Kempner. June 18, 1957. Isaac H. Kempner Collection. Rosenberg Library.

Letter from Johnny Mitchell to Balinese Members. March 1971. Rosenberg Library.

List or Manifest of Alien Passengers for the U.S. Immigration Officer at the Port of Arrival, New Orleans. April 21, 1904.

Script from WBAP-TV/NBC, Fort Worth, TX. June 21, 1957. UNT Libraries Special Collections.

Thirteenth Census of the United States: 1910—Population. Orleans County, New Orleans. Ancestry.com.

U.S. Department of Labor Petition for Naturalization to the United States of America. Salvatore Maceo, July 1, 1918. Ancestry.com

U.S. World War I Draft Registration Card. Salvatore Maceo. Ancestry.com.

U.S. World War I Draft Registration Card. Rosario Maceo. Ancestry.com.

INDEX

ABOUT THE AUTHOR

K imber Fountain is a native of the Texas Gulf Coast and longtime resident of Galveston Island. After earning a bachelor of arts degree in theatre and dance from the University of Texas at Austin, she lived in Chicago for several years before returning to Texas and making her home in Galveston, where she discovered a love for the city's rich history.

Her literary career began in 2012 as a writer for the *Island Guide,* and she has served as the editor-in-chief and feature writer for *Galveston Monthly* since 2015.

Kimber is a professional speaker who holds history and book lectures all over Texas, and in the spring of 2019, she created the Red Light District Tours of Galveston, a historical walking tour inspired by her books. Devoted to promoting and preserving the local Galveston arts community, Kimber served as chair of the Arts and Historic Preservation Advisory Board to the Galveston City Council for six years, and she is occasionally seen on stage at the Island East-End Theatre Company in downtown Galveston.

The Maceos and the Free State of Galveston is Kimber's third Galveston history book with The History Press; the *Galveston Seawall Chronicles* was released in 2017, followed by *Galveston's Red Light District: A History of the Line* in 2018.

For speaking engagements or information on the Red Light District Tours, email Kimber directly at kimber.fountain@gmail.com

Visit us at
www.historypress.com
....